Classic Southern
Desserts

from the editors of
Southern Living

Classic Southern
Desserts

All-time Favorite
Recipes for Cakes, Cookies,
Pies, Puddings, Cobblers,
Ice Cream & More

Oxmoor House®

©2010 by Oxmoor House, Inc.

Time Home Entertainment Inc.
135 West 50th Street, New York, NY 10020

ISBN-13: 978-0-8487-3643-9
ISBN-10: 0-8487-3643-5
Library of Congress Control Number: 2009937170

Printed in the United States of America
Third Printing 2012

Oxmoor House, Inc.
VP, Publishing Director: Jim Childs
Editorial Director: Susan Payne Dobbs
Senior Brand Manager: Daniel Fagan

CLASSIC SOUTHERN DESSERTS
Senior Editor: Rebecca Brennan
Project Editors: Emily Chappell, Sarah H. Doss
Senior Designer: Melissa Jones Clark
Director, Test Kitchens: Elizabeth Tyler Austin
Assistant Director, Test Kitchens: Julie Christopher
Test Kitchens Professionals: Allison E. Cox, Julie Gunter,
    Kathleen Royal Phillips, Catherine Crowell Steele,
    Ashley T. Strickland

Photography Director: Jim Bathie
Senior Photographers: Ralph Anderson, Van Chaplin,
    Gary Clark, Jennifer Davick, Art Meripol, Charles Walton IV
Photographers: Robbie Caponetto, Laura W. Glenn,
    Beth Dreiling Hontzas
Senior Photo Stylists: Kay E. Clarke, Buffy Hargett
Associate Photo Stylist: Katherine Eckert Coyne
Senior Production Manager: Greg Amason
Assistant Production Manager: Diane Rose

Contributors
Copy Editor: Dolores Hydock
Interns: Georgia Dodge, Natalie Heard, Laura Hoxworth,
    Perri K. Hubbard, Allison Sperando, Jessica Stephens,
    Christine Taylor

To order additional publications, call 1-800-765-6400 or
    1-800-491-0551.

For more books to enrich your life, visit **oxmoorhouse.com**

To search, savor, and share thousands of recipes, visit
myrecipes.com

Cover (left to right, top to bottom): Lemon Bars (page 104), Chocolate Icebox Pie (page 215), Chocolate-Key Lime Cupcake Pies (page 204), Banana Split Cake (page 65), Creamy Rice Pudding With Praline Sauce (page 303), Double-Crust Peach Cobbler (page 234)
Back cover (left to right): Ultimate Chocolate Pudding (page 307), Triple-Decker Strawberry Cake (page 42), Double Apple Pie With Cornmeal Crust (page 166)

Contents

Foreword

The reputations of many Southern cooks are tied to a fabulous dessert specialty. And, as we Southerners will agree, no meal is complete without a sweet finish. Whether you've been baking for years or are just starting out, this book of classic Southern desserts will guide your way to an abundance of guaranteed favorites.

Generations of home cooks pass down to us their best recipes, full of warm memories with family and friends. After much testing and sampling, we've selected our most highly rated favorites—a tough job, I can assure you.

We think you'll love Dark Chocolate Bundt Cake (page 61)—a moist and tender-crumbed slice of chocoholic bliss. Satisfy a weeknight craving with Too-Easy Cherry Cobbler (page 233). Its surprise, crisp, buttery white bread topping combines with canned cherries and a few pantry staples for simple goodness with little effort.

We've sprinkled our Food staff's expert knowledge and favorite techniques throughout these pages, sharing our most accurate and complete tips for baking success.

For example, you'll find everything you need to know to prevent common cake and pie mishaps in "Test Kitchens' Guide to Successful Baking" (page 332). Use these skills on our collection of delectable treats shared by our readers over the years.

No matter which recipes you choose to prepare, you'll capture a little bit of Southern charm and possibly bring back a bit of nostalgia with these fresh-baked desserts. So preheat your oven and get ready to delight your family and friends.

Scott Jones
Executive Editor

Luscious Layers & Other Cakes

We put a lot of love into these luscious layers. For a creamy coconut sensation, try the four-layer gem on page 46. We have included flavor profiles from velvety, rich chocolate and tangy lemon to buttery caramel and decadent banana. Pair them with our delicious frostings for incomparable desserts that will seal your reputation as a fantastic baker.

Call us shameless name droppers, but Southerners have a habit of honoring places and people, real or fictional, by naming cakes after them.

In the late 1800s, Emma Rylander Lane, of Clayton, Alabama, took first prize at a county fair with her sponge cake iced with a fluffy white frosting. She originally called the recipe Prize Cake, but friends convinced her to make the cake her namesake, and today you'll likely find Lane Cake served at a family's most noteworthy occasions. Along with Mrs. Lane, other cakes honoring people and places include Lord and Lady Baltimore Cakes, Martha Washington's Great Cake, and Kentucky Jam Cake. Other Southern-bred cakes include rich Caramel Cake, Coconut Cake, cocoa-based Red Velvet Cake, and, more recently, Hummingbird Cake. Submitted to *Southern Living* in 1978 from a North Carolina reader, Hummingbird Cake is the magazine's most requested recipe.

While a few of these cakes may rarely appear on today's tables, the art of cake baking remains a point of great pride among Southern cooks, and now, as in Colonial days, the type of cake served still conveys, to a degree, the status of the occasion—cakes made with available ingredients like everyday pound cakes and upside-down skillet cakes are for family; those made with previously hard-to-get ingredients like citrus fruit or coconut are reserved for weddings and holidays.

Double Chocolate-Praline-Fudge Cake, Fig Cake, and Lane Cake share a Southern heritage and definitely rank as cakes for "company."

New-Fashioned Blackberry Chocolate Spice Cake

Chocolate and spices mingle with sweet black-berries under a robe of chocolate fudge icing drizzled with blackberry sauce. Even traditionalists will be pleased with this updated classic.

makes 12 servings
prep: 35 min. • **cook: 30 min.** • **other: 1 hr., 10 min.**

1. Preheat oven to 350°. Grease 2 (9-inch) round cake pans, and dust with cocoa. Set aside.

2. Beat cake mix and next 11 ingredients at low speed with an electric mixer 1 minute; beat at medium speed 2 minutes. Fold in chopped chocolate. Pour batter into prepared pans.

3. Bake at 350° for 30 to 32 minutes or until a wooden pick inserted in center comes out clean. Let cool in pans on wire racks 10 minutes. Remove from pans to wire racks, and cool completely (about 1 hour). Wrap and chill cake layers 1 hour or up to 24 hours.

4. Using a serrated knife, slice cake layers in half horizontally to make 4 layers. Place 1 layer, cut side up, on cake plate. Spread one-third of blackberry filling over cake. Repeat procedure twice. Place final cake layer on top of cake, cut side down. Spread chocolate fudge frosting on top and sides of cake. Drizzle remaining filling over top of cake, letting it drip down sides of cake. Cover and chill in refrigerator until ready to serve. Just before serving, garnish, if desired.

Note: We tested with Betty Crocker for cake mix and Green and Black's Organic for bittersweet dark chocolate.

tip: As a general rule in cake baking, grease cake pans with shortening unless the recipe states otherwise.

Unsweetened cocoa
1   (18.25-oz.) package devil's food cake mix
1   (3.4-oz.) package chocolate instant pudding mix
3   large eggs
1¼ cups milk
1   cup canola oil
1   Tbsp. vanilla extract
1   tsp. chocolate extract
½   tsp. almond extract
2   tsp. ground cinnamon
¼   tsp. ground ginger
¼   tsp. ground nutmeg
¼   tsp. ground cloves
2   (3.5-oz.) bittersweet dark chocolate with orange and spices candy bars, chopped
1   (21-oz.) can blackberry pie filling
2   (16-oz.) cans chocolate fudge frosting
Garnish: fresh blackberries

Chocolate Turtle Cake

A simple sweet caramel filling and turtle candies sandwiched between fudgy brownielike cake layers and frosted with dark chocolate come together in this ultimate dessert splurge.

makes 12 servings
prep: 40 min. • **cook: 30 min.** • **other: 2 hr., 10 min.**

Unsweetened cocoa
1   (18.25-oz.) package devil's food cake mix
1   (3.9-oz.) package chocolate instant pudding mix
3   large eggs
1¼ cups milk
1   cup canola oil
2   tsp. vanilla extract
1   tsp. chocolate extract
1   tsp. instant coffee granules
1   (6-oz.) package semisweet chocolate morsels
1   cup chopped pecans
1   (16-oz.) container ready-to-spread cream cheese frosting
½   cup canned dulce de leche
2   (7-oz.) packages turtle candies
1   (16-oz.) can ready-to-spread chocolate fudge frosting
1   (12-oz.) jar dulce de leche ice cream topping
¼   cup pecan halves, toasted

1. Preheat oven to 350°. Grease 2 (9-inch) round cake pans, and dust with cocoa. Set aside.

2. Beat cake mix and next 7 ingredients at low speed with an electric mixer 1 minute; beat at medium speed 2 minutes. Fold in chocolate morsels and chopped pecans. Pour batter into pans.

3. Bake at 350° for 30 to 32 minutes or until a wooden pick inserted in center comes out clean. Let cool in pans on wire racks 10 minutes. Remove from pans to wire racks, and cool completely (about 1 hour). Wrap and chill cake layers at least 1 hour.

4. Whisk together cream cheese frosting and canned dulce de leche in a small bowl until well blended. Set aside. Cut 6 turtle candies in half, and set aside for garnish. Dice remaining turtle candies.

5. Using a serrated knife, slice cake layers in half horizontally to make 4 layers. Place 1 layer, cut side up, on cake plate. Spread with ½ cup cream cheese frosting mixture; sprinkle with one-third diced turtle candies. Repeat procedure twice. Place final cake layer on top of cake, cut side down. Spread chocolate fudge frosting on top and sides of cake. Cover and chill in refrigerator until ready to serve. Just before serving, drizzle dulce de leche ice cream topping over top of cake. Garnish with remaining halved turtle candies and pecan halves. Store in refrigerator.

Note: We tested with 2 dulce de leche products: canned and jarred. The canned product is by Nestlé and available in a 14-oz. can. It's quite thick, and when blended with ready-to-spread cream cheese frosting, makes a rich, caramel-flavored filling. Find it in the supermarket with the Mexican ingredients. The jarred dulce de leche ice cream topping is perfect to drizzle over the finished cake. Find it in the supermarket with other ice cream toppings.

Easy Black Forest Cake

Devil's food cake layers enriched with milk chocolate and a trio of extracts are sandwiched with the simplest and most decadent stuffing of them all—ready-to-eat cheesecake filling and cherry pie filling. Capped off with fudge frosting and gooey chocolate-covered cherries, this cake is a cinch to wow your guests.

makes 12 servings
prep: 35 min. • **cook: 30 min.** • **other: 2 hr., 10 min.**

1. Preheat oven to 350°. Grease 2 (9-inch) round cake pans, and dust with cocoa. Set aside.

2. Beat cake mix and next 7 ingredients at low speed with an electric mixer 1 minute; beat at medium speed 2 minutes. Fold in chopped chocolate. Pour batter into prepared pans.

3. Bake at 350° for 30 to 32 minutes or until a wooden pick inserted in center comes out clean. Let cool in pans on wire racks 10 minutes. Remove from pans to wire racks, and cool completely (about 1 hour). Wrap and chill cake layers 1 hour or up to 24 hours.

4. Using a serrated knife, slice cake layers in half horizontally to make 4 layers. Place 1 layer, cut side up, on cake plate. Spread one-third of cheesecake filling over cake; top with one-third of cherry pie filling. Repeat procedure twice with remaining cheesecake filling and cherry pie filling. Place final cake layer on top of cake, cut side down. Spread chocolate fudge frosting on top and sides of cake. Cover and chill in refrigerator until ready to serve. Garnish, if desired. Store in refrigerator.

Note: We tested with Philadelphia for ready-to-eat cheesecake filling. You'll find it in the dairy case with cream cheese products.

Unsweetened cocoa
1   (18.25-oz.) package devil's food
     cake mix
1   (3.4-oz.) package chocolate
     instant pudding mix
3   large eggs
1¼ cups milk
1   cup canola oil
1   Tbsp. vanilla extract
1½ tsp. chocolate extract
1   tsp. almond extract
3   (1.55-oz.) milk chocolate bars,
     chopped
1   (24.3-oz.) container ready-to-eat
     cheesecake filling, divided
1   (21-oz.) can cherry pie filling,
     divided
2   (16-oz.) cans chocolate fudge
     frosting
Garnish: chocolate-covered cherries,
     halved (optional)

Old-fashioned gingerbread is a homey dessert that combines the flavors of molasses, cinnamon, and ginger. Earlier generations of cooks commonly baked this "comfort food" dessert in a cast-iron skillet and served it with whipped cream. This updated version starts with a cake mix, and is ready to pop in the oven in just 15 minutes. Beer makes the cake super moist.

Gingerbread Cake With Stout Buttercream

makes 12 servings
prep: 15 min. • **cook: 35 min.** • **other: 1 hr., 10 min.**

1. Preheat oven to 350°. Stir together cake mix, eggs, and 2½ cups stout beer in a large bowl until combined. Pour batter evenly into 2 lightly greased 8-inch square pans.

2. Bake at 350° for 35 minutes or until a wooden pick inserted in center comes out clean. Let cool in pans on a wire rack 10 minutes. Remove from pans to wire rack, and cool completely (about 1 hour).

3. Beat softened butter at medium speed with an electric mixer until creamy. Gradually add powdered sugar and remaining ¼ cup stout beer, beating until blended after each addition. Beat 1 minute or until light and fluffy.

4. Spread stout buttercream between layers and on top of cake. Garnish, if desired.

Note: We tested with Betty Crocker Gingerbread Cake & Cookie Mix. We tested with Terrapin Wake-n-Bake Coffee Oatmeal Imperial Stout at one testing and Guinness Extra Stout beer at another.

2   (14.5-oz.) packages gingerbread
     cake mix
2   large eggs
2 ¾ cups stout beer, at room
     temperature, divided
½   cup butter, softened
1   (16-oz.) package powdered sugar
Garnishes: toasted pecans, rosemary
     sprigs

Fig Cake

makes 6 to 8 servings
prep: 20 min. • **cook: 43 min.** • **other: 1 hr., 10 min.**

1   cup chopped pecans
3   large eggs
1   cup sugar
1   cup vegetable oil
½   cup buttermilk
1   tsp. vanilla extract
2   cups all-purpose flour
1   tsp. baking soda
1   tsp. salt
1   tsp. ground cinnamon
½   tsp. ground cloves
½   tsp. ground nutmeg
½   cup fig preserves
½   cup applesauce
Honey-Cream Cheese Frosting
Garnishes: dried figs, fresh mint
       sprigs

1. Preheat oven to 350˚. Arrange pecans in a single layer in a shallow pan. Bake 8 minutes or until toasted and fragrant.

2. Beat eggs, sugar, and oil at medium speed with an electric mixer until blended. Add buttermilk and vanilla; beat well.

3. Combine flour and next 5 ingredients; gradually add to buttermilk mixture, beating until blended. Fold in fig preserves, applesauce, and toasted pecans. (Batter will be thin.) Pour into 2 greased and floured 8-inch round cake pans.

4. Bake at 350˚ for 35 to 40 minutes or until a wooden pick inserted in center comes out clean. Let cool on wire racks 10 minutes. Remove from pans to wire racks, and cool completely (about 1 hour).

5. Spread Honey-Cream Cheese Frosting between layers and on top and sides of cake. Store cake in refrigerator. Garnish, if desired.

Note: We tested with Braswell's Fig Preserves. Coarsely chop figs in preserves, if necessary.

Honey-Cream Cheese Frosting:

makes 3 ½ cups
prep: 10 min.

1 ½   (8-oz.) packages cream cheese,
       softened
⅓   cup butter, softened
1 ½   Tbsp. honey
2   cups sifted powdered sugar

1. Beat cream cheese, butter, and honey at medium speed with an electric mixer just until smooth. Gradually add powdered sugar, beating at low speed just until blended.

Decadent Banana Cake With Coconut-Cream Cheese Frosting

makes 8 to 10 servings
prep: 15 min. • **cook: 30 min.** • **other: 1 hr., 10 min.**

1. Preheat oven to 350°. Sift together cake flour, baking soda, and salt.

2. Beat butter at medium speed with an electric mixer until creamy. Add granulated sugar and brown sugar; beat until light and fluffy. Add eggs, 1 at a time, beating until blended after each addition.

3. Beat in bananas at low speed. Gradually add flour mixture to butter mixture alternately with buttermilk, beginning and ending with flour mixture. Beat at medium speed just until blended after each addition. Pour batter into 2 greased and floured 9-inch round cake pans.

4. Bake at 350° for 30 minutes or until a wooden pick inserted in center comes out clean. Let cool in pans on wire racks 10 minutes. Remove from pans to wire racks, and cool completely (about 1 hour).

5. Spread Coconut-Cream Cheese Frosting between layers and on top and sides of cake. Garnish, if desired.

2 ½ cups plus 5 ½ Tbsp. cake flour
1 Tbsp. baking soda
Pinch of salt
½ cup unsalted butter, softened
1 cup granulated sugar
¾ cup firmly packed light brown sugar
2 large eggs
4 large ripe bananas, mashed (about 2 cups)
⅔ cup buttermilk
Coconut-Cream Cheese Frosting
Garnish: dried banana chips

Coconut-Cream Cheese Frosting:

makes about 3 cups
prep: 10 min.

1. Beat cream cheese and butter at medium speed with an electric mixer until creamy. Gradually add powdered sugar alternately with milk, beating at low speed until blended. Add vanilla; beat until smooth. Stir in coconut.

1 (8-oz.) package cream cheese, softened
2 Tbsp. butter, softened
3 ½ cups powdered sugar, sifted
2 tsp. milk
½ tsp. vanilla extract
1 ¼ cups sweetened flaked coconut

Caramel Cake

makes 8 servings
prep: 15 min. • **cook: 30 min.** • **other: 1 hr., 10 min.**

1   (8-oz.) carton sour cream
¼   cup milk
1   cup butter, softened
2   cups sugar
4   large eggs
2 ¾ cups all-purpose flour
2   tsp. baking powder
½   tsp. salt
1   tsp. vanilla extract
Caramel Frosting

1. Preheat oven to 350°. Combine sour cream and milk.

2. Beat butter at medium speed with an electric mixer until creamy; gradually add sugar, beating well. Add eggs, 1 at a time, beating after each addition.

3. Combine flour, baking powder, and salt; add to butter mixture alternately with sour cream mixture, beginning and ending with flour mixture. Beat at medium-low speed until blended after each addition. Stir in vanilla. Pour batter into 2 greased and floured 9-inch round cake pans.

4. Bake at 350° for 30 to 35 minutes or until a wooden pick inserted in center comes out clean. Let cool in pans on wire racks 10 minutes. Remove from pans to wire racks, and cool completely (about 1 hour).

5. Spread Caramel Frosting between layers and on top and sides of cake.

Caramel Frosting:

makes 3 cups
prep: 30 min. • **cook: 20 min.** • **other: 1 hr.**

⅓   cup sugar
1   Tbsp. all-purpose flour
2 ½ cups sugar
1   cup milk
¾   cup butter
1   tsp. vanilla extract

1. Sprinkle ⅓ cup sugar in a shallow, heavy 3½-qt. Dutch oven; cook over medium heat, stirring constantly, 3 minutes or until sugar is melted and syrup is light golden brown (sugar will clump). Remove from heat.

2. Stir together 1 Tbsp. flour and 2½ cups sugar in a large saucepan; add milk, and bring to a boil over medium-high heat, stirring constantly.

3. Gradually pour about one-fourth hot milk mixture into cara-melized sugar, stirring constantly; gradually stir in remaining hot milk mixture until smooth. (Mixture will lump, but continue stirring until smooth.)

4. Cover and cook over low heat 2 minutes. Increase heat to medium; uncover and cook, without stirring, until a candy

thermometer reaches 238° (soft ball stage, about 10 minutes). Add butter, stirring until blended. Remove from heat and let stand, without stirring, until temperature drops to 110° (about 1 hour).

5. Pour into bowl of a heavy-duty electric stand mixer. Add vanilla, and beat at medium speed (setting 4) with whisk attachment until spreading consistency (about 20 minutes).

Note: We tested with a KitchenAid 300-watt Ultra Power heavy-duty electric stand mixer.

It may be hard to imagine today, but chocolate was not used as a food ingredient until the early 1800s. Before then, it was used as a beverage and even as a cure for spasms and obesity, among other illnesses.

Chocolate Layer Cake With Vanilla Buttercream Frosting

Food Editor Mary Allen Perry developed this "choco-licious" dessert temptation. The addition of hot tap water at the end makes for an exceptionally moist cake.

makes 8 servings
prep: 40 min. • **cook: 45 min.** • **other: 1 hr., 10 min.**

1 ½   cups semisweet chocolate morsels
½   cup butter, softened
1   (16-oz.) package light brown sugar
3   large eggs
2   cups all-purpose flour
1   tsp. baking soda
½   tsp. salt
1   (8-oz.) container sour cream
1   cup hot water
2   tsp. vanilla extract
Vanilla Buttercream Frosting
Garnishes: white and dark chocolate shavings and curls

1. Preheat oven to 350˚. Melt chocolate morsels in a microwave-safe bowl at HIGH 1½ minutes or until melted and smooth, stirring at 30-second intervals.

2. Beat butter and brown sugar at medium speed with an electric mixer until well blended (about 5 minutes). Add eggs, 1 at a time, beating just until blended after each addition. Add melted chocolate, beating just until blended.

3. Sift together flour, baking soda, and salt. Gradually add to chocolate mixture alternately with sour cream, beginning and ending with flour mixture. Beat at low speed just until blended after each addition. Gradually add 1 cup hot water in a slow, steady stream, beating at low speed just until blended. Stir in vanilla.

4. Spoon batter into 2 greased and floured 9-inch round, 2-inch-deep cake pans.

5. Bake at 350˚ for 40 to 45 minutes or until a wooden pick inserted in center comes out clean. Let cool in pans on wire racks 10 minutes. Remove from pans to wire racks, and cool completely (about 1 hour).

6. Spread Vanilla Buttercream Frosting between layers and on top and sides of cake. Garnish, if desired.

Note: If your cake pans are only 1½ inches deep, use 3 pans, and reduce baking time to 25 to 30 minutes.

Vanilla Buttercream Frosting:

makes 6 cups
prep: 10 min.

1. Beat butter at medium speed with an electric mixer until creamy; gradually add powdered sugar alternately with milk, beating at low speed until blended after each addition. Stir in 1 Tbsp. vanilla.

Bourbon Buttercream Frosting: Substitute ⅓ cup bourbon and ⅓ cup milk for ⅔ cup milk. Proceed with recipe as directed.

1	cup butter, softened
1	(32-oz.) package powdered sugar
⅔	cup milk
1	Tbsp. vanilla extract

Basic White Cake

makes 12 servings
prep: 15 min. • **cook: 25 min.** • **other: 6 hr., 25 min.**

½ cup butter, softened

½ cup shortening

2 cups sugar

3 cups cake flour

4 tsp. baking powder

½ tsp. salt

⅔ cup milk

2 tsp. vanilla extract

¾ tsp. almond extract

6 egg whites

Milk Chocolate Frosting

Garnish: rainbow candy sprinkles

1. Preheat oven to 325°. Beat butter and shortening at medium speed with an electric mixer until creamy; gradually add sugar, beating well.

2. Combine flour, baking powder, and salt; add to butter mixture alternately with milk and ⅔ cup water, beginning and ending with flour mixture. Beat at low speed until blended after each addition. Stir in extracts.

3. Beat egg whites at high speed until stiff peaks form; fold about one-third of egg whites into batter. Gradually fold in remaining egg whites. Pour batter into 3 greased and floured 8-inch round cake pans.

4. Bake at 325° for 25 to 30 minutes or until a wooden pick inserted in center comes out clean. Let cool in pans on wire racks 10 minutes. Remove from pans to wire racks, and let cool 15 minutes. Wrap in plastic wrap. Freeze 4 hours.

5. Unwrap frozen cake layers. Spread Milk Chocolate Frosting between layers and on top and sides of cake. Let stand at room temperature 2 hours before serving. Garnish, if desired.

To fold in egg whites, gently guide a rubber spatula down 1 side and along bottom of bowl.

Draw spatula up through center of batter, folding some of batter up and over egg whites.

Rotate bowl a quarter turn. Continue folding, rotating bowl, just until the egg whites are incorporated.

Milk Chocolate Frosting:

makes 4 cups
prep: 10 min.

1. Beat butter at medium speed with an electric mixer until creamy. Add remaining ingredients, beating until smooth.

1	cup butter, softened
6	cups powdered sugar
⅓	cup unsweetened cocoa
½	cup milk

Heavenly Candy Bar Cake

kids love it

makes 12 servings
prep: 15 min. • **cook: 35 min.** • **other: 1 hr., 10 min.**

1. Preheat oven to 350°. Melt candy bars and ½ cup butter in a heavy saucepan over low heat, stirring constantly, until smooth.

2. Beat sugar and remaining 1 cup butter at medium speed with an electric mixer 3 minutes or until well blended. Add eggs, 1 at a time, beating just until blended after each addition.

3. Combine flour and salt. Whisk together buttermilk and baking soda. Gradually add flour mixture to sugar mixture alternately with buttermilk mixture, beginning and ending with flour mixture. Beat at low speed just until blended after each addition. Stir in melted candy bar mixture and vanilla. Spoon batter into 3 greased and floured 9-inch round cake pans.

4. Bake at 350° for 25 to 30 minutes or until a wooden pick inserted in center comes out clean. Let cool in pans on wire racks 10 minutes. Remove from pans to wire racks, and cool completely.

5. Spread half of Chocolate-Marshmallow Frosting between cake layers. Spread remaining frosting evenly over top and sides of cake. Garnish, if desired.

Note: We tested with Milky Way Bars.

9	fun-size or 21 mini chocolate-coated caramel-and-creamy nougat bars
1½	cups butter, softened and divided
2	cups sugar
3	large eggs
2½	cups all-purpose flour
1	tsp. salt
1½	cups buttermilk
½	tsp. baking soda
1	tsp. vanilla extract
	Chocolate-Marshmallow Frosting
	Garnish: chopped frozen fun-size or mini chocolate-coated caramel-and-creamy nougat bars

Chocolate-Marshmallow Frosting:

makes 4½ cups
prep: 15 min. • **cook: 5 min.**

1. Melt first 4 ingredients in a 2-qt. saucepan over medium-low heat, stirring constantly, until mixture is melted and smooth.

2. Transfer chocolate mixture to a large bowl. Place bowl into a larger bowl filled with ice and water. Gradually add powdered sugar alternately with 4 Tbsp. milk, beating at low speed with an electric mixer until blended after each addition. Increase speed to medium-high, and beat 5 minutes or until frosting is cool, thick, and spreadable, adding up to 2 Tbsp. additional milk, if necessary, for desired consistency. Stir in vanilla. Use immediately.

3	cups miniature marshmallows
¾	cup butter, cut up
¾	cup evaporated milk
6	oz. unsweetened chocolate, chopped
6	cups powdered sugar
4	to 6 Tbsp. milk
1	Tbsp. vanilla extract

chocolate decadence

Vegetable cooking spray

Wax paper

1   cup butter

¼   cup unsweetened cocoa

½   cup buttermilk

2   large eggs

1   tsp. baking soda

1   tsp. vanilla extract

2   cups sugar

2   cups all-purpose flour

½   tsp. salt

Chocolate Ganache

Praline Frosting

Double Chocolate-Praline-Fudge Cake

This cake is off-the-charts rich. If you like pralines, you'll love this candylike frosting.

makes 12 servings
prep: 35 min. ○ **cook: 24 min.** ○ **other: 2 hr., 13 min.**

1. Preheat oven to 350°. Coat 3 (8-inch) round cake pans with cooking spray; line with wax paper.

2. Cook butter, cocoa, and 1 cup water in a saucepan over low heat, whisking constantly, 2 minutes or until butter is melted and mixture is smooth; remove from heat. Let cool.

3. Meanwhile, beat buttermilk and next 3 ingredients at medium speed with an electric mixer until combined. Add cocoa mixture to buttermilk mixture, beating until blended.

4. Combine sugar, flour, and salt; gradually add to buttermilk mixture, beating until blended after each addition. (Batter will be thin.) Pour batter into prepared pans.

5. Bake at 350° for 22 to 24 minutes or until set. Let cool in pans on wire racks 10 minutes. Remove from pans to wire racks, and let cool completely (about 1 hour).

6. Spread about ½ cup Chocolate Ganache between each cake layer; spread a thin layer of ganache on sides of cake. Chill cake 3 minutes. Spread remaining ganache on sides of cake. Chill 30 minutes.

7. Prepare Praline Frosting. Pour Praline Frosting slowly over center of cake, spreading to edges, allowing some frosting to run over sides. Let stand 30 minutes, allowing frosting to harden.

Chocolate Ganache:

makes 2 cups
prep: 5 min.

1. Microwave whipping cream in a 2-cup glass measuring cup at HIGH 2 minutes. Add chocolate morsels, stirring until melted and smooth.

1	cup whipping cream
1	(12-oz.) package semisweet chocolate morsels

Praline Frosting:

makes about 1¾ cups
prep: 8 min. • **cook: 11 min.**

1. Preheat oven to 350°. Arrange pecans in a single layer in a shallow pan. Bake 8 to 10 minutes, stirring occasionally.

2. Bring brown sugar, whipping cream, and butter to a boil in a 2-qt. saucepan over medium heat, stirring often; boil 1 minute. Remove from heat, and whisk in powdered sugar and vanilla until smooth. Stir in toasted pecans, stirring gently, 3 to 5 minutes or until mixture begins to cool and thicken slightly. Use immediately.

1	cup chopped pecans
1	cup firmly packed brown sugar
⅓	cup whipping cream
¼	cup butter
1	cup powdered sugar
1	tsp. vanilla extract

tip:

Ganache (gahn-AHSH) is a rich frosting made with chocolate and whipping cream.

- Ganache can be served warm, as a glaze.
- It can be cooled slightly and used as a filling for cakes, cookies, or tarts.
- After chilling for several hours, ganache becomes firm enough to shape into truffles.

Hummingbird Cake is the most requested recipe in *Southern Living* history. The recipe first appeared in the magazine in 1978 as a reader recipe submitted by Mrs. L. H. Wiggins of Greensboro, North Carolina; since then it's been the star at the table at family gatherings across the South. This updated version has less sugar and oil than the original, fewer eggs, and half the salt.

Updated Hummingbird Cake

makes 12 servings
prep: 20 min. • **cook: 23 min.** • **other: 1 hr., 10 min.**

3   cups all-purpose flour
1¾ cups sugar
1   tsp. baking soda
1   tsp. ground cinnamon
½   tsp. salt
2   large eggs
1   (8-oz.) can crushed pineapple, undrained
1¾ cups mashed ripe banana (about 5 to 6 bananas)
½   cup unsweetened applesauce
3   Tbsp. vegetable oil
1½ tsp. vanilla extract
5-Cup Lemon-Cream Cheese Frosting (page 35)
Garnish: chopped walnuts

1. Preheat oven to 350°. Combine flour and next 4 ingredients in a large bowl. Stir together eggs and next 5 ingredients; add to flour mixture, stirring just until dry ingredients are moistened. (Do not beat.) Pour batter into 3 greased and floured 9-inch round cake pans.

2. Bake at 350° for 23 to 25 minutes or until a wooden pick inserted in center comes out clean. Let cool in pans on wire racks 10 minutes. Remove from pans to wire racks, and cool completely (about 1 hour).

3. Spread 5-Cup Lemon-Cream Cheese Frosting between layers and on top and sides of cake. Garnish, if desired.

Red Velvet Layer Cake

Classic Red Velvet Cake holds happy memories
for many people. Nowadays, there are Red Velvet
cupcakes, cookies, cheesecakes, and sheet cakes,
too. But at the end of the day, the three-layer cake
stands tall and reigns supreme.

makes 12 servings
prep: 15 min. • **bake: 18 min.** • **other: 1 hr., 10 min.**

1. Preheat oven to 350°. Beat butter at medium speed with an
electric mixer until creamy. Gradually add sugar, beating until
light and fluffy. Add eggs, 1 at a time, beating just until blended
after each addition.

2. Stir together flour, cocoa, and baking soda. Add to butter mixture alternately with sour cream, beginning and ending with flour
mixture. Beat at low speed just until blended after each addition.
Stir in vanilla; stir in red food coloring. Spoon cake batter into
3 greased and floured 8-inch round cake pans.

3. Bake at 350° for 18 to 20 minutes or until a wooden pick
inserted in center comes out clean. Let cool in pans on wire racks
10 minutes. Remove from pans to wire racks, and cool completely
(about 1 hour).

4. Spread 5-Cup Cream Cheese Frosting between layers and on
top and sides of cake.

1	cup butter, softened
2 ½	cups sugar
6	large eggs
3	cups all-purpose flour
3	Tbsp. unsweetened cocoa
¼	tsp. baking soda
1	(8-oz.) container sour cream
2	tsp. vanilla extract
2	(1-oz.) bottles red food coloring
1 ½	recipes 5-Cup Cream Cheese Frosting

5-Cup Cream Cheese Frosting:

makes about 5 cups
prep: 10 min.

1. Beat cream cheese and butter at medium speed with an electric
mixer until creamy. Gradually add powdered sugar, beating until
fluffy. Stir in vanilla.

5-Cup Lemon-Cream Cheese Frosting: Reduce vanilla to 1 tsp.
Beat in 2 tsp. lemon zest and 1 Tbsp. fresh lemon juice before
stirring in vanilla.

2	(8-oz.) packages cream cheese, softened
½	cup butter, softened
1	(32-oz.) package powdered sugar
2	tsp. vanilla extract

Italian Cream Cake

makes 20 servings
prep: 15 min. • **cook: 25 min.** • **other: 1 hr., 10 min.**

½ cup butter, softened
½ cup shortening
2 cups sugar
5 large eggs, separated
1 Tbsp. vanilla extract
2 cups all-purpose flour
1 tsp. baking soda
1 cup buttermilk
1 cup sweetened flaked coconut
Nutty Cream Cheese Frosting
Garnish: toasted pecan halves

1. Preheat oven to 350°. Beat butter and shortening in a large mixing bowl at medium speed with an electric mixer until creamy; gradually add sugar, beating well. Add egg yolks, 1 at a time, beating until blended after each addition. Add vanilla; beat just until blended.

2. Combine flour and baking soda; add to butter mixture alternately with buttermilk, beginning and ending with flour mixture. Beat at low speed just until blended after each addition. Stir in coconut.

3. Beat egg whites until stiff peaks form; fold into batter. Pour batter into 3 greased and floured 9-inch round cake pans.

4. Bake at 350° for 25 minutes or until a wooden pick inserted in center comes out clean. Let cool in pans on wire racks 10 minutes. Remove from pans to wire racks, and cool completely (about 1 hour).

5. Spread Nutty Cream Cheese Frosting between layers and on top and sides of cake. Garnish, if desired.

tip:

To separate eggs, have 3 bowls on hand: 1 to break each egg over, 1 for yolks, and a third for egg whites. This way, if the yolk cracks as you break the egg, you won't lose the other whites you have separated.

Hold cracked egg over a bowl; pull apart eggshell halves, keeping the yolk in 1 half. Gently transfer yolk back and forth between shell halves, allowing white to drip into bowl.

Gently place egg yolk in a second bowl.

Check egg white for traces of yolk; if clean, transfer white into a third bowl. Repeat with remaining eggs, breaking eggs 1 at a time over the first bowl.

Nutty Cream Cheese Frosting:

makes about 4 cups
prep. 10 min. • **cook: 8 min.**

1. Preheat oven to 350°. Arrange pecans in a single layer in a shallow pan. Bake 8 to 10 minutes or until toasted and fragrant, stirring occasionally. Let cool.

2. Meanwhile, beat cream cheese, butter, and vanilla at medium speed with an electric mixer until creamy. Add powdered sugar, beating at low speed until blended. Beat frosting at high speed until smooth; stir in toasted pecans.

1   cup chopped pecans
1   (8-oz.) package cream cheese, softened
½   cup butter, softened
1   Tbsp. vanilla extract
1   (16-oz.) package powdered sugar, sifted

This cake, namesake of Emma Rylander Lane of Clayton, Alabama, has graced Southern tables since the recipe appeared in Lane's self-published cookbook, *Some Good Things to Eat,* in 1898. It's still considered a traditional "celebration" cake in the South.

Lane Cake

makes 12 servings
prep: 20 min. • cook: 25 min. • other: 1 hr., 10 min.

1. Preheat oven to 325°. Beat butter at medium speed with an electric mixer until creamy; gradually add sugar, beating well. Combine flour, baking powder, and salt; add to butter mixture alternately with milk, beginning and ending with flour mixture. Beat at low speed just until blended after each addition.

2. Beat egg whites at high speed until stiff peaks form. Fold one-third of egg whites into batter; fold in remaining egg whites. Spoon batter into 3 greased and floured 9-inch round cake pans.

3. Bake at 325° for 25 minutes or until a wooden pick inserted in center comes out clean. Let cool in pans on wire racks 10 minutes. Remove from pans to wire racks, and cool completely (about 1 hour).

4. Spread Lane Cake Filling between layers and on top of cake. Prepare 7-Minute Frosting; spread onto sides of cake.

1   cup unsalted butter, softened
2   cups sugar
3 ½ cups all-purpose flour
1   Tbsp. baking powder
¼   tsp. salt
1   cup milk
8   egg whites
Lane Cake Filling
½   recipe 7-Minute Frosting

Lane Cake Filling:

makes 5 cups
prep: 15 min. • **cook: 35 min.** • **other: 1 hr.**

1. Pour water to a depth of 1½ inches into a 3½-qt. saucepan over medium-high heat; bring to a boil. Reduce heat to medium, and simmer.

2. Beat egg yolks at medium speed with an electric mixer 3 minutes; gradually add sugar, beating until blended. Beat 3 minutes. Gradually add butter, beating at low speed until blended.

3. Transfer mixture to a 3-qt. heatproof bowl. Place bowl over simmering water. Cook, stirring constantly, until mixture thickens and an instant-read thermometer registers 170° (about 30 to 35 minutes). Remove from heat; stir in pecans and remaining ingredients. Let cool 1 hour.

12	egg yolks
1½	cups sugar
¾	cup unsalted butter, melted
1½	cups finely chopped pecans
1½	cups finely chopped raisins
1½	cups sweetened flaked coconut
½	cup bourbon
1½	tsp. vanilla extract

7-Minute Frosting:

This classic frosting that's cooked over a double boiler for approximately seven minutes has a light and fluffy marshmallowlike texture.

makes 4½ cups
prep: 13 min. • **cook: 7 min.**

1. Pour water to a depth of 1½ inches into a 3½-qt. saucepan over medium-high heat; bring to a boil. Reduce heat to medium, and simmer.

2. Combine first 3 ingredients in a 3-qt. heat-proof bowl; beat at low speed with a handheld electric mixer until blended. Place bowl over simmering water, beating at high speed 7 minutes or until soft peaks form; remove from heat. Add vanilla. Beat to spreading consistency (about 3 to 5 minutes). Spread immediately.

4	egg whites
2	cups sugar
½	cup water
2	tsp. vanilla extract

Toasted Almond Butter Cake

makes 12 servings
prep: 25 min. • **cook: 26 min.** • **other: 1 hr., 20 min.**

1. Preheat oven to 350°. Arrange almonds in a single layer in a shallow pan. Bake 6 minutes or until toasted and fragrant. Let cool 10 minutes. Reserve ½ cup almonds; chop remaining almonds.

2. Beat butter at medium speed with an electric mixer until creamy. Gradually add sugar, beating well. Add egg yolks, 1 at a time, beating until blended after each addition.

3. Combine flour and baking soda; add to butter mixture alternately with buttermilk, beginning and ending with flour mixture. Beat at low speed just until blended after each addition. Stir in almond extract, coconut, and chopped almonds.

4. Beat egg whites at high speed until stiff peaks form; fold into batter. Pour batter into 3 greased and floured 9-inch round cake pans.

5. Bake at 350° for 20 to 22 minutes or until a wooden pick inserted in center comes out clean. Let cool in pans on wire racks 10 minutes. Remove from pans to wire racks, and cool completely (about 1 hour).

6. Spread 5-Cup Cream Cheese Frosting between layers and on top and sides of cake. Sprinkle with reserved ½ cup slivered almonds.

1 ½ cups slivered almonds
½   cup butter, softened
2   cups sugar
5   large eggs, separated
2 ¼ cups all-purpose flour
1 ¼ tsp. baking soda
1   cup plus 2 Tbsp. buttermilk
1   tsp. almond extract
1   cup sweetened flaked coconut
5-Cup Cream Cheese Frosting
     (page 35)

Mama Dip's Carrot Cake

This recipe from Chapel Hill, North Carolina restaurateur Mildred "Mama Dip" Council makes one of the best carrot cakes we've tasted. The cake layers can be prepared ahead and frozen up to one month.

makes 12 servings
prep: 30 min. • **cook: 47 min.** • **other: 1 hr., 10 min.**

1. Preheat oven to 350°. Arrange walnuts in a single layer in a shallow pan. Bake 12 minutes or until toasted and fragrant.

2. Sift together flour, cinnamon, and baking soda. Line bottoms of 3 lightly greased 9-inch round cake pans with parchment paper; lightly grease parchment paper.

3. Beat sugar and oil at medium speed with an electric mixer until smooth. Add eggs, 1 at a time, beating until blended after each addition. Add flour mixture, beating at low speed just until blended. Fold in carrots and 1 cup toasted walnuts. Spoon batter into prepared pans.

4. Bake at 350° for 35 to 40 minutes or until a wooden pick inserted in center comes out clean. Let cool in pans on wire racks 10 minutes. Remove from pans to wire racks; remove parchment paper, and let cakes cool completely (about 1 hour).

5. Spread frosting between layers and on top and sides of cake; sprinkle remaining 1 cup chopped walnuts halfway up sides of cake.

bake & freeze

2   cups chopped walnuts
2 ½ cups self-rising flour
1 ½ tsp. ground cinnamon
1   tsp. baking soda
Parchment paper
2   cups sugar
1   cup vegetable oil
4   large eggs
3   cups grated carrots
5-Cup Cream Cheese Frosting
    (page 35)

1   (18.25-oz.) package white
      cake mix
1   (3-oz.) package strawberry
      gelatin
4   large eggs
½   cup sugar
½   cup finely chopped fresh
      strawberries
½   cup milk
½   cup vegetable oil
⅓   cup all-purpose flour
Strawberry Buttercream Frosting
Garnish: whole and halved
      strawberries

Triple-Decker Strawberry Cake

This cake from Anne Byrn, aka The Cake Mix Doctor, is so good no one will know it's not made from scratch. We doubled the frosting called for in Anne's original recipe to add extra richness.

makes 12 servings
prep: 25 min. • **cook: 23 min.** • **other: 1 hr., 10 min.**

1. Preheat oven to 350°. Beat cake mix and next 7 ingredients at low speed with an electric mixer 1 minute. Scrape down sides, and beat at medium speed 2 more minutes, stopping to scrape down sides, as needed. (Strawberries should be well blended.)

2. Pour batter into 3 greased and floured 9-inch round cake pans.

3. Bake at 350° for 23 minutes or until cakes spring back when pressed lightly with a finger. Let cool in pans on wire racks 10 minutes. Remove from pans, and cool completely (about 1 hour).

4. Spread Strawberry Buttercream Frosting between layers and on top and sides of cake. Garnish, if desired. Serve immediately, or chill up to 1 week.

Note: We tested with Betty Crocker SuperMoist Cake Mix, White. Recipe for Strawberry Tart (shown opposite, lower right) is on page 186.

To make ahead: Prepare recipe as directed. Chill, uncovered, 20 minutes or until frosting is set. Cover well with wax paper, and store in refrigerator up to 1 week. To freeze, wrap chilled frosted cake with aluminum foil, and freeze up to 6 months. Thaw in the refrigerator 24 hours.

Strawberry Buttercream Frosting:

1   cup butter, softened
1   (32-oz.) package powdered sugar,
      sifted
1   cup finely chopped fresh
      strawberries

makes 2½ cups
prep: 10 min.

1. Beat butter at medium speed with an electric mixer until fluffy (about 20 seconds). Add sugar and strawberries, beating at low speed until creamy. (Add more sugar if frosting is too thin, or add strawberries if too thick.)

Luscious Lemon Cake

For a more elegant presentation, frost the entire cake.

makes 12 servings
prep: 20 min. • **cook: 12 min.** • **other: 1 hr., 10 min.**

1. Preheat oven to 375°. Beat egg yolks at high speed with an electric mixer 4 minutes or until thick and pale. Set aside.

2. Beat butter at medium speed until creamy; gradually add sugar, beating well. Add beaten egg yolks, beating well.

3. Combine flour, baking powder, and salt; add to butter mixture alternately with milk, beginning and ending with flour mixture. Beat at low speed just until blended after each addition. Stir in 1 tsp. lemon zest, 1 tsp. fresh lemon juice, and 1 tsp. vanilla. Spoon batter into 3 greased and floured 8-inch round cake pans.

4. Bake at 375° for 12 to 17 minutes or until a wooden pick inserted in center comes out clean. Let cool in pans on wire racks 10 minutes. Remove from pans to wire racks, and cool completely (about 1 hour).

5. Spread Luscious Lemon Frosting between layers and on top of cake. Cover and chill until ready to serve.

8	egg yolks
¾	cup butter, softened
1¼	cups sugar
2½	cups cake flour
1	Tbsp. baking powder
¼	tsp. salt
¾	cup milk
1	tsp. lemon zest
1	tsp. fresh lemon juice
1	tsp. vanilla extract
	Luscious Lemon Frosting

Luscious Lemon Frosting:

makes 4 cups
prep: 10 min.

1. Beat butter at medium speed with an electric mixer until creamy; stir in lemon zest and juice. (Mixture will appear curdled.) Gradually add sugar; beat at high speed 4 minutes or until spreading consistency. Gradually beat in up to 2 Tbsp. half-and-half, if necessary, for desired consistency.

1	cup butter, softened
2	tsp. lemon zest
¼	cup fresh lemon juice
1	(32-oz.) package powdered sugar
1	to 2 Tbsp. half-and-half (optional)

Four-Layer Coconut Cake

makes 14 to 16 servings
prep: 45 min. • **cook: 28 min.** • **other: 1 hr., 10 min.**

3   cups all-purpose flour
2 ⅔ cups sugar
1 ½ cups butter, softened
1   cup milk
1   tsp. baking powder
½   tsp. salt
2   tsp. coconut extract
1   tsp. vanilla extract
5   large eggs
1   (6-oz.) package frozen flaked
    coconut, thawed
1   cup coconut shavings
Coconut Filling
2   cups whipping cream
¼   cup powdered sugar

1. Preheat oven to 400°. Beat first 6 ingredients at medium speed with an electric mixer until well blended. Add extracts, beating well. Add eggs, 1 at a time, beating until blended after each addition. Stir in flaked coconut. Pour batter into 4 greased and floured 9-inch round cake pans.

2. Bake at 400° for 20 minutes or until a wooden pick inserted in center comes out clean. Let cool in pans on wire racks 10 minutes. Remove from pans to wire racks, and cool completely (about 1 hour).

3. Meanwhile, reduce oven temperature to 350°. Arrange coconut shavings in a single layer in a shallow pan. Bake 8 to 10 minutes or until toasted, stirring occasionally.

4. Spread Coconut Filling between layers, leaving a 1-inch border. Beat whipping cream at high speed until foamy. Gradually add powdered sugar, beating until soft peaks form. Spread on top and sides of cake. Sprinkle toasted coconut on top and sides of cake, pressing gently to adhere.

Coconut Filling:

makes 5½ cups
prep: 10 min. • **cook: 12 min.** • **other: 30 min.**

2   cups sugar
2   cups milk
4   large eggs, lightly beaten
¼   cup all-purpose flour
2   (6-oz.) packages frozen flaked
    coconut, thawed
2   tsp. vanilla extract

1. Cook first 4 ingredients in a large saucepan over medium-low heat, whisking constantly, 12 to 15 minutes or until thickened and bubbly. Remove from heat, and stir in coconut and vanilla. Let cool 30 minutes or until completely cool.

tip:

Coconut shavings can be purchased in the bulk section of your local health food store or dried fruit section in the supermarket.

Cooks in the Appalachians found a great way to use dried sweet apples as filling for cakes with up to eight thin layers. Some cooks poured batter into cake pans to bake, and others rolled out the dough and cut it into rounds. In earlier days, the stack cake was used as a wedding cake. Guests would bring a layer, adding to layers already started on a plate. It was said that the taller the finished stack, the more popular the bride.

Apple Stack Cake

Don't be tempted to eat the cake until it has stood for two days. This standing time allows the moisture from the filling to seep throughout the cake and fill it with moist, slightly spicy goodness.

makes 12 to 16 servings
prep: 23 min. • **cook: 30 min.** • **other: 2 days**

⅓   cup shortening
½   cup sugar
1   large egg
4   cups all-purpose flour
1   tsp. baking powder
1   tsp. baking soda
½   tsp. salt
½   cup buttermilk
½   cup molasses
2 ½ tsp. sugar
Dried Apple Filling

1. Preheat oven to 400°. Beat shortening at medium speed with an electric mixer 2 minutes or until creamy. Gradually add ½ cup sugar, beating 5 to 7 minutes. Add egg, beating until yellow disappears.

2. Combine flour and next 3 ingredients. Stir together buttermilk and molasses in a large measuring cup. Gradually add flour mixture to shortening mixture alternately with buttermilk mixture, beginning and ending with flour mixture. Beat at low speed just until blended after each addition.

3. Divide dough into 5 equal portions; place each portion in a 9-inch round greased and floured cake pan, and firmly press with floured fingers into pan. Prick dough several times with a fork. Sprinkle each layer evenly with ½ tsp. sugar.

4. Bake at 400° for 10 minutes or until golden brown. (Only bake layers on 1 rack at a time.) Repeat procedure as needed to bake in

pans. Remove layers from pans to wire racks, and cool completely.

5. Spread 1½ cups Dried Apple Filling between each layer to within ½ inch of edge, beginning and ending with a cake layer. (Save your prettiest cake layer for the top.) Loosely cover cake, and let stand 2 days at room temperature.

Dried Apple Filling:

makes 6 cups
prep: 5 min. • **cook: 50 min.**

1. Stir together apples and 6 cups water in a large saucepan or Dutch oven. Bring to a boil; reduce heat, and simmer 30 minutes or until tender. Stir in sugar, and, if desired, spices. Return mixture to a boil; reduce heat, and simmer, stirring occasionally, 10 to 15 minutes or until most of liquid has evaporated. Let cool completely.

3	6-oz.) packages dried sliced apples
1	cup firmly packed brown sugar
1	tsp. ground ginger (optional)
1	tsp. ground cinnamon (optional)
½	tsp. ground allspice (optional)
½	tsp. ground nutmeg (optional)

kids love it

2   (16-oz.) containers fresh
      strawberries, sliced or quartered
¾   cup sugar, divided
¼   tsp. almond extract (optional)
1   cup whipping cream
2   Tbsp. sugar
2 ¾ cups all-purpose flour
4   tsp. baking powder
¾   cup cold butter, cut up
2   large eggs, lightly beaten
1   (8-oz.) container sour cream
1   tsp. vanilla extract
Vegetable cooking spray
Garnish: fresh strawberries with
      leaves

Classic Strawberry Shortcake

This summertime favorite shows off juicy strawberries like no other dessert, though sliced peaches are equally nice as an option.

makes 8 servings
prep: 20 min. • **cook: 12 min.** • **other: 2 hr.**

1. Combine strawberries, ½ cup sugar, and, if desired, almond extract. Cover berry mixture, and let stand 2 hours.

2. Beat whipping cream at medium speed with an electric mixer until foamy; gradually add 2 Tbsp. sugar, beating until soft peaks form. Cover and chill up to 2 hours.

3. Preheat oven to 450°. Combine flour, remaining ¼ cup sugar, and baking powder in a large bowl; cut butter into flour mixture with a pastry blender or 2 forks until crumbly.

4. Whisk together eggs, sour cream, and vanilla until blended; add to flour mixture, stirring just until dry ingredients are moistened. Drop dough by lightly greased ⅓ cupfuls onto a lightly greased baking sheet. (Coat cup with cooking spray after each drop.)

5. Bake at 450° for 12 to 15 minutes or until golden.

6. Split shortcakes in half horizontally. Spoon about ½ cup berry mixture onto each shortcake bottom; top each with a rounded tablespoon of chilled whipped cream and a shortcake top. Serve with remaining whipped cream. Garnish, if desired.

tip:

If your berries are really sweet, decrease the sugar to suit your taste. Drop the dough easily by using a lightly greased ⅓-cup dry measure.

The name "Pound Cake" traditionally was given to a cake recipe whose ingredients consisted of 1 pound of eggs, 1 pound of flour, 1 pound of sugar, and 1 pound of butter—the result was said to be a perfectly balanced cake.

Million-Dollar Pound Cake

makes 10 to 12 servings
prep: 30 min. • **cook: 1 hr., 40 min.** • **other: 1 hr., 10 min.**

1. Preheat oven to 300°. Generously grease and lightly flour a 10-inch (14-cup) tube pan. Beat butter at medium speed with an electric mixer until light yellow in color and creamy. Gradually add sugar, beating at medium speed until light and fluffy. Add eggs, 1 at a time, beating just until yellow disappears.

2. Add flour to butter mixture alternately with milk, beginning and ending with flour. Beat at low speed just until blended after each addition. (Batter should be smooth.) Stir in extracts. Pour batter into prepared pan.

3. Bake at 300° for 1 hour and 40 minutes or until a long wooden pick inserted in center comes out clean. Let cool in pan on a wire rack 10 to 15 minutes. Remove from pan to wire rack, and cool completely (about 1 hour).

1	lb. butter, softened
3	cups sugar
6	large eggs
4	cups all-purpose flour
¾	cup milk
1	tsp. almond extract
1	tsp. vanilla extract

Cream Cheese Pound Cake

Cream Cheese Pound Cake

This delicately crumbed cake received the highest possible recipe rating from our Test Kitchens staff.

makes 10 servings
prep: 15 min. • **cook: 1 hr., 40 min.** • **other: 1 hr., 10 min.**

1. Preheat oven to 300°. Beat butter and cream cheese at medium speed with an electric mixer until creamy; gradually add sugar, beating well. Add eggs, 1 at a time, beating until combined.

2. Combine flour and salt; gradually add to butter mixture, beating at low speed just until blended after each addition. Stir in vanilla. Pour batter into a greased and floured 10-inch Bundt pan.

3. Bake at 300° for 1 hour and 40 minutes or until a wooden pick inserted in center comes out clean. Let cool in pan on a wire rack 10 to 15 minutes. Remove from pan to wire rack, and cool completely (about 1 hour).

1 ½	cups butter, softened
1	(8-oz.) package cream cheese, softened
3	cups sugar
6	large eggs
3	cups all-purpose flour
Dash of salt	
1	Tbsp. vanilla extract

Ginger Pound Cake

makes 10 to 12 servings
prep: 23 min. • **cook: 1 hr., 30 min.** • **other: 1 hr., 15 min.**

1. Preheat oven to 325°. Cook milk and ginger in a saucepan over medium heat 5 minutes or until thoroughly heated (do not boil). Remove from heat, and let stand 10 to 15 minutes.

2. Beat butter at medium speed with an electric mixer until creamy; gradually add sugar, beating 5 to 7 minutes. Add eggs, 1 at a time, beating just until yellow disappears after each addition.

3. Add flour to butter mixture alternately with milk mixture, beginning and ending with flour. Beat at low speed just until blended after each addition. Stir in vanilla. Pour batter into a greased and floured 10-inch (16-cup) tube pan.

4. Bake at 325° for 1 hour and 25 minutes or until a wooden pick inserted in center comes out clean. Let cool in pan on a wire rack 10 minutes. Remove from pan to wire rack, and cool completely (about 1 hour). Serve with ice cream. Garnish, if desired.

¾	cup milk
1	(2.7-oz.) jar crystallized ginger, finely minced
2	cups butter, softened
3	cups sugar
6	large eggs
4	cups all-purpose flour
1	tsp. vanilla extract
Vanilla bean ice cream	
Garnish: crystallized ginger	

Banana Pound Cake

This moist, full-flavored banana cake needs no ice cream or sauce to enhance its appeal. But if you insist, we recommend pralines-and-cream ice cream.

makes 10 to 12 servings
prep: 18 min. • **bake: 1 hr., 20 min.** • **other: 1 hr., 10 min.**

1 ½   cups butter, softened
3   cups sugar
5   large eggs
3   ripe bananas, mashed
3   Tbsp. milk
2   tsp. vanilla extract
3   cups all-purpose flour
1   tsp. baking powder
½   tsp. salt
¾   cup chopped pecans

1. Preheat oven to 350°. Beat butter at medium speed with an electric mixer about 2 minutes or until creamy. Gradually add sugar, beating 5 to 7 minutes. Add eggs, 1 at a time, beating just until yellow disappears after each addition.

2. Combine mashed bananas, milk, and vanilla.

3. Combine flour, baking powder, and salt; add to batter alternately with banana mixture, beginning and ending with flour mixture. Beat at low speed just until blended after each addition. Pour into a greased and floured 10-inch tube pan. Sprinkle with pecans.

4. Bake at 350° for 1 hour and 20 minutes or until a long wooden pick inserted in center of cake comes out clean. Let cool in pan on a wire rack 10 to 15 minutes. Remove from pan to wire rack, and cool completely (about 1 hour).

holiday favorite

2 cups finely chopped pecans, divided
1 lb. butter, softened
3 cups sugar
6 large eggs
4 cups all-purpose flour
⅛ tsp. salt
¾ cup milk
2 Tbsp. orange zest
2 tsp. ground cinnamon
1 tsp. ground nutmeg
1 tsp. vanilla extract
1 tsp. lemon extract
1 tsp. orange extract
½ tsp. ground cloves
Orange Syrup
Glazed Pecan Halves (optional)
Garnish: halved orange slices

Orange-Pecan-Spice Pound Cake

Sprinkle chopped pecans into the buttered tube pan before spooning in the batter to form a nice, crisp coating on top of this pound cake.

makes 10 to 12 servings
prep: 35 min. • **cook: 1 hr., 40 min.** • **other: 1 hr., 20 min.**

1. Preheat oven to 350°. Arrange pecans in a single layer in a shallow pan, and bake 10 minutes or until toasted and fragrant, stirring after 5 minutes. Reduce oven temperature to 300°.

2. Sprinkle 1¼ cups toasted pecans into a generously buttered 10-inch tube pan; shake to evenly coat bottom and sides of pan. (Excess nuts will fall to bottom of pan. Make sure nuts are in an even layer in bottom of pan.)

3. Beat butter at medium speed with an electric mixer until creamy; gradually add sugar, beating well. Add eggs, 1 at a time, beating until blended after each addition.

4. Combine flour and salt; add to butter mixture alternately with milk, beginning and ending with flour mixture. Beat at low speed until blended after each addition. Stir in orange zest, next 6 ingredients, and remaining ¾ cup pecans. Spoon batter into prepared pan.

5. Bake at 300° for 1 hour and 30 minutes to 1 hour and 40 minutes or until a long wooden pick inserted in center comes out clean. Let cool in pan on a wire rack 20 minutes. Remove cake from pan; invert cake, pecan crust-side-up, onto wire rack.

6. Prepare Orange Syrup. Brush top and sides of pound cake gently several times with hot Orange Syrup, using a 2-inch-wide pastry brush and allowing the cake to absorb the Orange Syrup after each brushing. (Do not pour syrup over the cake.) Let cake cool completely (about 1 hour). Arrange Glazed Pecan Halves around cake, if desired. Garnish, if desired.

Orange Syrup:

makes 1 cup
prep: 5 min. • **cook: 8 min.**

1. Grate zest from orange to equal about 2 Tbsp. Cut orange in half; squeeze juice from orange into a measuring cup to equal ½ cup.

2. Stir together orange zest, juice, and sugar in a small saucepan over low heat. Cook, stirring frequently, 3 minutes or until sugar is dissolved. Increase heat to medium-high. Bring mixture to a boil, stirring constantly, and boil 3 minutes. Use immediately.

1   large orange
1   cup sugar

Glazed Pecan Halves:

makes 2 cups
prep: 5 min. • **cook: 20 min.** • **other: 1 hr.**

1. Preheat oven to 350°. Stir together pecan halves and corn syrup, stirring to coat pecans. Line a 15- x 10-inch jelly-roll pan with parchment paper or aluminum foil; coat with cooking spray. Arrange pecans in an even layer in pan.

2. Bake at 350° for 12 minutes; stir using a rubber spatula. Bake 8 more minutes. Remove from oven, and stir. Arrange in a single layer on wax paper. Let cool completely (about 1 hour).

2   cups pecan halves
⅓   cup light corn syrup
Parchment paper
Vegetable cooking spray
Wax paper

For Glazed Pecan Halves, stir together pecans and corn syrup.

Arrange pecans in a single layer on a parchment paper-lined pan.

After baking, quickly remove glazed pecans from pan with a spatula onto wax paper before they harden.

The recipe for Bananas Foster was created in the 1950s by Paul Blangé, chef at Brennan's restaurant in New Orleans. The original recipe was spooned over vanilla ice cream; our version adds Louisiana flavor to rum pound cake.

1   cup butter, softened

3   cups sugar, divided

6   large eggs, separated

3   cups all-purpose flour

¼   tsp. baking soda

1   (8-oz.) container sour cream

1   tsp. vanilla extract

1   tsp. lemon extract

Buttered Rum Glaze

Bananas Foster Sauce

Buttered Rum Pound Cake With Bananas Foster Sauce

makes 10 to 12 servings
prep: 29 min. • cook: 1 hr., 30 min. • other: 4 hr., 10 min.

1. Preheat oven to 325°. Beat butter at medium speed with a heavy-duty electric stand mixer until creamy. Add 2½ cups sugar, beating 4 to 5 minutes or until fluffy. Add egg yolks, 1 at a time, beating just until yellow disappears.

2. Combine flour and baking soda; add to butter mixture alternately with sour cream, beginning and ending with flour mixture. Beat at medium speed just until blended after each addition. Stir in extracts.

3. Beat egg whites until foamy; gradually add remaining ½ cup sugar, 1 Tbsp. at a time, beating until stiff peaks form. Fold into batter. Pour batter into a greased and floured 10-inch (16-cup) tube pan.

4. Bake at 325° for 1 hour and 30 minutes or until a long wooden pick inserted in center comes out clean. Let cool in pan 10 to 15 minutes. Remove from pan, and place on a serving plate. While warm, prick cake surface at 1-inch intervals with a wooden pick; spoon warm Buttered Rum Glaze over cake. Let stand, covered, at least 4 hours or overnight. Serve with Bananas Foster Sauce.

Lemon Pound Cake: Prepare recipe as directed through Step 3, adding 2 Tbsp. lemon zest to batter. Proceed with recipe as directed. Omit Buttered Rum Glaze; do not serve with sauce.

Buttered Rum Glaze:

makes 1¼ cups
prep: 5 min. • **cook: 10 min.**

1. Preheat oven to 350°. Arrange pecans in a single layer in a shallow pan, and bake 5 minutes or until toasted and fragrant.

2. Combine butter, rum, sugar, and 3 Tbsp. water in a small saucepan; bring to a boil. Boil, stirring constantly, 3 minutes. Remove from heat, and stir in pecans.

½	cup chopped pecans
6	Tbsp. butter
3	Tbsp. light rum
¾	cup sugar

Bananas Foster Sauce:

makes 8 servings
prep: 5 min. • **cook: 8 min.**

1. Melt butter in a large skillet over medium heat; add next 3 ingredients. Cook, stirring constantly, 3 minutes or until bubbly. Add bananas, and cook 2 to 3 minutes or until thoroughly heated. Remove from heat.

2. Heat rum in a small saucepan over medium heat (do not boil). Remove saucepan from heat; quickly pour rum over banana mixture, and carefully ignite the fumes just above the mixture with a long match or long multipurpose lighter. Let flames die down; serve immediately with Buttered Rum Pound Cake.

¼	cup butter
½	cup firmly packed brown sugar
⅓	cup banana liqueur
¼	tsp. ground cinnamon
4	bananas, peeled and sliced
⅓	cup light rum

Stirring constantly, cook butter, brown sugar, banana liqueur, and cinnamon until bubbly.

Add bananas, and cook 2 to 3 minutes or until heated.

Remove banana mixture from heat. Pour rum mixture over banana mixture, and carefully ignite with a long match.

The Bundt® pan was created by Nordic Ware® and trademarked in 1950 by H. David Dalquist, the founder of Nordic Ware. Since the pan's introduction, the company has sold more than 50 million Bundt pans.

Dark Chocolate Bundt Cake

makes 12 servings
prep: 20 min. • **cook: 1 hr., 20 min.** • **other: 1 hr., 15 min.**

1. Preheat oven to 325°. Melt chocolate in a microwave-safe bowl at HIGH for 30-second intervals until melted (about 1½ minutes total). Stir in chocolate syrup until smooth.

2. Beat butter at medium speed with an electric mixer until creamy. Gradually add sugar, beating at medium speed until light and fluffy. Add eggs, 1 at a time, beating just until blended after each addition.

3. Sift together flour, baking soda, and salt. Add to butter mixture alternately with buttermilk, beginning and ending with flour mixture. Beat at low speed just until blended after each addition. Stir in vanilla and melted chocolate just until blended. Pour batter into a greased and floured 14-cup Bundt pan.

4. Bake at 325° for 1 hour and 20 minutes or until a long wooden pick inserted in center comes out clean. Let cool in pan on a wire rack 15 minutes. Remove from pan to wire rack, and cool completely (about 1 hour). Garnish, if desired.

1 (8-oz.) package semisweet chocolate baking squares, coarsely chopped
1 (16-oz.) can chocolate syrup
1 cup butter, softened
2 cups sugar
4 large eggs
2 ½ cups all-purpose flour
½ tsp. baking soda
¼ tsp. salt
1 cup buttermilk
1 tsp. vanilla extract
Garnish: powdered sugar

tip:

To ensure the Bundt cake releases easily from the pan, use a pastry brush to generously coat the inside with solid vegetable shortening. Then sprinkle with flour, tilting and tapping the pan to evenly cover all the narrow crevices. If the pan has a nonstick coating, a vegetable cooking spray made especially for baking, such as Pam Baking or Crisco with Flour, works equally well.

Praline Bundt Cake

makes 12 servings
prep: 30 min. • **cook: 1 hr., 20 min.** • **other: 1 hr., 15 min.**

1. Preheat oven to 350°. Arrange 1 cup pecans in a single layer on a baking sheet. Bake at 350° for 5 to 7 minutes or until toasted and fragrant. Let cool on a wire rack 15 minutes or until completely cool. Reduce oven temperature to 325°.

2. Beat butter and cream cheese at medium speed with an electric mixer until creamy. Gradually add brown sugar, beating until well blended. Add eggs, 1 at a time, beating just until blended after each addition.

3. Sift together flour and next 3 ingredients. Add to butter mixture alternately with sour cream, beginning and ending with flour mixture. Beat batter at low speed just until blended after each addition. Stir in toasted pecans and vanilla. Spoon batter into a greased and floured 12-cup Bundt pan.

4. Bake at 325° for 1 hour and 15 minutes or until a long wooden pick inserted in center comes out clean. Let cool in pan on a wire rack 15 minutes. Remove from pan to wire rack, and cool completely (about 1 hour).

5. Prepare Praline Icing, and spoon immediately over cake. Sprinkle top of cake with Sugared Pecans.

1	cup chopped pecans
1	cup butter, softened
1	(8-oz.) package cream cheese, softened
1	(16-oz.) package dark brown sugar
4	large eggs
2 ½	cups all-purpose flour
1	tsp. baking powder
½	tsp. baking soda
¼	tsp. salt
1	(8-oz.) container sour cream
2	tsp. vanilla extract
Praline Icing	
Sugared Pecans	

Praline Icing:

makes about 1½ cups
prep: 8 min. • **cook: 5 min.**

1	cup firmly packed light brown sugar	¼	cup milk
½	cup butter	1	cup powdered sugar, sifted
		1	tsp. vanilla extract

1. Bring first 3 ingredients to a boil in a 2-qt. saucepan over medium heat, whisking constantly; boil 1 minute. Remove from heat; whisk in powdered sugar and vanilla until smooth. Stir gently 3 to 5 minutes or until mixture begins to cool and thickens slightly. Use immediately.

Sugared Pecans:

makes about 5 cups
prep: 10 min. • **cook: 18 min.** • **other: 30 min.**

1. Whisk egg white until foamy; add pecans, and stir until evenly coated.

2. Stir together sugars until blended; sprinkle sugar mixture over pecans. Stir gently until pecans are evenly coated. Spread pecans in a single layer in a lightly greased aluminum foil-lined 15- x 10-inch jelly-roll pan.

3. Bake at 350° for 18 to 20 minutes or until pecans are toasted and dry, stirring once after 10 minutes. Remove from oven, and let cool 30 minutes or until completely cool.

Note: Store pecans in a zip-top plastic freezer bag at room temperature up to 3 days or freeze up to 3 weeks.

1	egg white
4	cups pecan halves (about 1 lb.)
⅓	cup granulated sugar
⅓	cup firmly packed light brown sugar

tip:

Measured Success. Cake recipes often yield different amounts of batter, so it's a good idea to double check the size of your Bundt pan by filling it to the rim with cups of water. Depending on the brand, a 10-inch pan may hold 10, 12, or 14 cups. If you use a smaller pan than is called for in a recipe, fill the pan no more than one-half to two-thirds full. Refrigerate the remaining batter up to 1½ hours, return to room temperature, and bake as cupcakes or miniature loaf cakes.

Honey-Apple Cake

makes 12 servings
prep: 25 min. • **cook: 55 min.** • **other: 1 hr., 15 min.**

1. Preheat oven to 350°. Grease and flour a 12-cup Bundt pan; sprinkle bottom of pan with ¼ cup pecans.

2. Beat sugar, oil, and honey at medium speed with an electric mixer until well blended. Add eggs, 1 at a time, beating just until blended.

3. Combine flour and next 4 ingredients. Gradually add to sugar mixture, beating at low speed just until blended. Stir in vanilla, remaining ¾ cup pecans, and chopped apples. Spoon batter over pecans in pan.

4. Bake at 350° for 55 to 60 minutes or until a long wooden pick inserted in center comes out clean. Let cool in pan on a wire rack 15 minutes. Remove from pan, and place on wire rack over wax paper. Pour ½ cup Honey Sauce over warm cake. Let cool completely (about 1 hour). Heat remaining Honey Sauce; serve cake with sauce and, if desired, ice cream.

Honey Sauce:

makes 1½ cups
prep: 5 min. • **cook: 8 min.**

1 cup firmly packed light brown sugar	¼ cup milk
½ cup butter	¼ cup clover honey

1. Bring all ingredients to a boil in a medium saucepan over medium-high heat, stirring constantly; boil, stirring constantly, 5 minutes.

---

1 cup chopped pecans, divided
2 cups sugar
1 cup vegetable oil
¼ cup clover honey
3 large eggs
3 cups all-purpose flour
1 tsp. baking soda
1 tsp. salt
1 tsp. ground cinnamon
¼ tsp. ground nutmeg
1 tsp. vanilla extract
2 Golden Delicious apples, peeled and chopped (about 3 cups)
Wax paper
Honey Sauce
Vanilla ice cream (optional)

Banana Split Cake

makes 10 to 12 servings
prep: 30 min. • **cook: 1 hr.** • **other: 1 hr., 10 min.**

kids love it

1. Preheat oven to 350°. Combine first 4 ingredients in a large bowl. Stir together eggs, oil, and buttermilk. Add oil mixture to flour mixture, stirring just until dry ingredients are moistened. Stir in banana and next 3 ingredients.

2. Drain pineapple, reserving 2 Tbsp. liquid. Gently press pineapple and maraschino cherries between layers of paper towels. Chop cherries. Stir pineapple and cherries into banana mixture. Spoon into a greased and floured 10-inch tube pan.

3. Bake at 350° for 1 hour or until a wooden pick inserted in center comes out clean. Let cool in pan on a wire rack 10 to 15 minutes. Remove from pan to wire rack, and cool completely (about 1 hour).

4. Beat cream cheese at medium speed with an electric mixer until smooth. Gradually add powdered sugar, beating at low speed until blended. Stir in reserved pineapple juice. Pour over cake; garnish, if desired.

3	cups all-purpose flour
2	cups sugar
1	tsp. baking soda
¼	tsp. salt
3	large eggs
1	cup vegetable oil
½	cup buttermilk
2	cups mashed banana (5 medium)
1	cup chopped pecans
1	cup flaked coconut
1½	tsp. vanilla extract
1	(20-oz.) can crushed pineapple, undrained
1	(16-oz.) jar maraschino cherries, drained
1	(8-oz.) package cream cheese, softened
1½	cups powdered sugar

Garnishes: grated milk chocolate, chopped pecans, hot fudge sauce

Celebration Cake

makes 24 servings
prep: 25 min. • **cook: 30 min.** • **other: 1 hr., 40 min.**

1. Preheat oven to 350°. Beat sugar and butter at medium speed with an electric mixer until creamy. Add eggs, 1 at a time, beating until yellow disappears after each addition. Beat in lemon juice and vanilla.

2. Combine flour and baking soda in a small bowl; add to sugar mixture alternately with buttermilk, beginning and ending with flour mixture. Beat at medium speed just until blended after each addition. Pour batter into a greased and floured 13- x 9-inch pan.

3. Bake at 350° for 30 to 35 minutes or until a wooden pick inserted in center comes out clean. Let cool in pan on a wire rack 10 minutes. Remove from pan to wire rack, and cool completely (about 1 hour). Wrap in plastic wrap, and freeze 30 minutes.

4. Unwrap cake, and place on a serving platter. Reserve ½ cup Celebration Cream Cheese Frosting for decorations, and spread top and sides of cake with remaining frosting. Decorate as desired.

Celebration Cream Cheese Frosting:

makes 3½ cups
prep: 5 min.

1. Beat together all ingredients at medium speed with an electric mixer until fluffy.

tip:

Decorative Options. Alternate orange, green, and yellow candy-coated chewy fruit candies around edge of cake. Arrange miniature alphabet cookies on cake as desired. Tint half of reserved ½ cup frosting with green liquid food coloring, stirring until blended. Tint remaining half with yellow liquid food coloring. Outline letters on alphabet cookies using desired frosting. Dollop remaining frosting onto cake. Arrange additional candy-coated chewy fruit candies on cake. We tested with Tropical Skittles for candies and Nabisco 100 Calorie Pack Alpha-Bits Mini Cookies.

holiday favorite

2	cups sugar
1	cup butter
2	large eggs
2	tsp. fresh lemon juice
1	tsp. vanilla extract
2 ½	cups cake flour
½	tsp. baking soda
1	cup buttermilk

Celebration Cream Cheese Frosting
Decorative Options (at right)

½	cup butter, softened
1	(8-oz.) package cream cheese, softened
1	(3-oz.) package cream cheese, softened
1	(16-oz.) package powdered sugar
2	tsp. fresh lemon juice

Grandma's Hint-of-Mint Chocolate Cake

When you're bringing dessert for a potluck dinner, this is the cake to take. Garnish it with a few chocolate-covered peppermint patty candies to give a hint of the flavor.

makes 12 servings
prep: 25 min. • **cook: 45 min.**

1. Preheat oven to 350°. Combine first 4 ingredients in a large bowl; set aside.

2. Combine butter and 1 cup water in a saucepan; cook over low heat just until butter melts. Remove from heat; stir in baking soda. Add to flour mixture, stirring well.

3. Combine egg, buttermilk, and vanilla; stir into flour mixture. Pour batter into a greased and floured 13- x 9-inch pan. Bake at 350° for 40 minutes.

4. Top with peppermint patties, and bake 2 to 3 more minutes or until patties melt. Gently spread melted patties over top of cake. Let cool completely. Spread Chocolate Frosting over top of cake. Garnish, if desired.

Chocolate Frosting:

makes 2 cups
prep: 5 min. • **cook: 3 min.**

1. Combine butter and milk in a saucepan; cook over low heat until butter melts and mixture is hot. Remove from heat. Combine powdered sugar and cocoa in a large bowl; add butter mixture, stirring until smooth. Stir in vanilla.

tip:

A handy disposable 13- x 9-inch foil pan with a tight-fitting lid makes baking, transport, and cleanup easy.

2	cups all-purpose flour
2	cups sugar
¼	cup unsweetened cocoa
1	tsp. ground cinnamon
1	cup butter
1	tsp. baking soda
1	large egg, lightly beaten
½	cup buttermilk
1	tsp. vanilla extract
1	(12-oz.) package miniature chocolate-covered peppermint patties, unwrapped and halved crosswise

Chocolate Frosting
Garnish: miniature chocolate-covered peppermint patties

½	cup butter
⅓	cup milk
1	(16-oz.) package powdered sugar, sifted
¼	cup unsweetened cocoa
1	tsp. vanilla extract

Chocolate Marble Sheet Cake

This cake's rich, creamy frosting blends coffee with cocoa for a delightful mocha flavor.

makes 12 servings
prep: 20 min. • **cook: 23 min.** • **other: 1 hr.**

1   cup butter, softened

1 ¾ cups sugar, divided

2   large eggs

2   tsp. vanilla extract

2 ½ cups all-purpose flour

1   Tbsp. baking powder

½   tsp. salt

1   cup half-and-half

¼   cup unsweetened cocoa

3   Tbsp. hot water

Mocha Frosting

1. Preheat oven to 325°. Beat butter and 1½ cups sugar at medium speed with a heavy-duty electric stand mixer 4 to 5 minutes or until creamy. Add eggs, 1 at a time, beating just until blended after each addition. Beat in vanilla.

2. Sift together flour, baking powder, and salt. Add to butter mixture alternately with half-and-half, beginning and ending with flour mixture. Beat at low speed just until blended after each addition, stopping to scrape bowl as needed.

3. Spoon 1¼ cups batter into a 2-qt. bowl, and stir in cocoa, 3 Tbsp. hot water, and remaining ¼ cup sugar until well blended.

4. Spread remaining vanilla batter into a greased and floured 15- x 10-inch jelly-roll pan. Spoon chocolate batter onto vanilla batter in pan; gently swirl with a knife or small spatula.

5. Bake at 325° for 23 to 28 minutes or until a wooden pick inserted in center comes out clean. Let cool completely in pan on a wire rack (about 1 hour). Spread top of cake with Mocha Frosting.

To make Chocolate Marble Sheet Cake, spread vanilla batter evenly in pan.

Spoon mounds of chocolate batter over vanilla batter in pan.

Using a knife or small spatula, swirl the two batters together.

Mocha Frosting:

makes 2⅓ cups
prep: 10 min.

1. Whisk together sugar and cocoa in a medium bowl. Combine coffee and vanilla.

2. Beat butter at medium speed with a heavy-duty electric stand mixer until creamy; gradually add sugar mixture alternately with coffee mixture, beating at low speed until blended. Beat in half-and-half, 1 Tbsp. at a time, until smooth and mixture has reached desired consistency.

Mocha-Almond Frosting: Decrease vanilla extract to 1 tsp. Proceed with recipe as directed, adding ½ tsp. almond extract to coffee mixture in Step 1.

3	cups powdered sugar
⅔	cup unsweetened cocoa
3	Tbsp. hot brewed coffee
2	tsp. vanilla extract
½	cup butter, softened
3	to 4 Tbsp. half-and-half

chocolate decadence

¾   cup chopped pecans

1   cup cola soft drink

½   cup buttermilk

1   cup butter, softened

1¾ cups sugar

2   large eggs, lightly beaten

2   tsp. vanilla extract

2   cups all-purpose flour

¼   cup unsweetened cocoa

1   tsp. baking soda

1½ cups miniature marshmallows

Classic Cola Frosting

Classic Cola Cake

Don't make the frosting ahead—you need to pour it over the cake shortly after baking.

makes 12 servings
prep: 10 min. • **cook: 38 min.** • **other: 10 min.**

1. Preheat oven to 350°. Arrange chopped pecans in a single layer in a shallow pan. Bake 8 to 9 minutes or until toasted and fragrant.

2. Combine cola and buttermilk.

3. Beat butter at low speed with an electric mixer until creamy. Gradually add sugar, beating until blended. Add eggs and vanilla; beat at low speed just until blended.

4. Combine flour, cocoa, and baking soda. Add to butter mixture alternately with cola mixture, beginning and ending with flour mixture. Beat at low speed just until blended after each addition. Stir in marshmallows. Pour batter into a greased and floured 13- x 9-inch pan.

5. Bake at 350° for 30 to 35 minutes. Remove from oven; cool 10 minutes.

6. Pour Classic Cola Frosting over warm cake; sprinkle with toasted pecans.

Classic Cola Frosting:

makes 2¼ cups
prep: 10 min. • **cook: 5 min.**

½ cup butter	1 (16-oz.) package powdered
⅓ cup cola soft drink	sugar
3 Tbsp. unsweetened cocoa	1 Tbsp. vanilla extract

1. Bring first 3 ingredients to a boil in a large saucepan over medium heat, stirring until butter is melted. Remove from heat; whisk in sugar and vanilla. Use immediately.

Texas Sheet Cake

Food historians can't agree on why this sheet cake came to be called "Texas," but on one thing they do concur: It's as easy to make as it is delicious.

makes 24 servings
prep: 20 min. • **cook: 35 min.**

1. Preheat oven to 325°. Stir together sugar, flour, baking soda, and salt in a large bowl; stir in sour cream and lightly beaten eggs.

2. Melt butter in a heavy saucepan over medium heat. Whisk in 1 cup water and ¼ cup cocoa. Bring to a boil, whisking constantly. Remove from heat.

3. Stir cocoa mixture into sour cream mixture. Pour batter into a lightly greased 15- x 10-inch jelly-roll pan.

4. Bake at 325° for 25 to 30 minutes or until a wooden pick inserted in center of cake comes out clean. Spread Fudge Frosting evenly over warm cake.

Peanut Butter-Fudge Cake: Substitute 1½ cups creamy peanut butter and ½ cup buttermilk for sour cream. Proceed with recipe as directed, increasing bake time to 30 to 35 minutes or until a wooden pick inserted in center comes out clean.

Fudge Frosting:

makes about 2 cups
prep: 10 min. • **cook: 5 min.**

½ cup butter
⅓ cup unsweetened cocoa
⅓ cup milk
1 (16-oz.) package powdered sugar
1 tsp. vanilla extract

1. Stir together first 3 ingredients in a medium saucepan over medium heat. Cook, stirring constantly, 3 minutes or until butter is melted. Cook, stirring constantly, 2 minutes or until slightly thickened; remove from heat. Beat in powdered sugar and vanilla at medium-high speed with an electric mixer until smooth.

chocolate decadence

2 cups sugar
2 cups all-purpose flour
1 tsp. baking soda
½ tsp. salt
1 (8-oz.) container sour cream
2 large eggs, lightly beaten
1 cup butter
¼ cup unsweetened cocoa
Fudge Frosting

tip:
Make the frosting right before taking the cake out of the oven, and spread it on the warm cake.

Just like the banks of the Mississippi River, this cake is ooey, gooey, and chocolate brown. The original Mississippi mud cake is thought to have been created by World War II-era cooks who found a way to use available ingredients to make a dense chocolate cake.

Mississippi Mud Cake

makes 15 servings
prep: 15 min. • **cook: 36 min.**

1. Preheat oven to 350°. Place pecans in a single layer in a shallow pan. Bake 8 to 10 minutes or until toasted and fragrant.

2. Microwave 1 cup butter and chocolate bar in a large microwave-safe glass bowl at HIGH 1 minute, stirring at 30-second intervals. Whisk sugar and next 5 ingredients into chocolate mixture. Pour batter into a greased 15- x 10-inch jelly-roll pan.

4. Bake at 350° for 20 minutes. Remove from oven, and sprinkle evenly with miniature marshmallows; bake 8 to 10 more minutes or until golden brown. Drizzle warm cake with Chocolate Frosting, and sprinkle evenly with toasted pecans.

Note: We tested with Duncan Hines Chocolate Lover's Double Fudge Brownie Mix.

1	cup chopped pecans
1	cup butter
1	(4-oz.) semisweet chocolate baking bar, chopped
2	cups sugar
1 ½	cups all-purpose flour
½	cup unsweetened cocoa
4	large eggs
1	tsp. vanilla extract
¾	tsp. salt
1	(10.5-oz.) bag miniature marshmallows
	Chocolate Frosting

Chocolate Frosting:

makes 3 cups
prep: 10 min. • **cook: 5 min.**

1. Melt butter in a saucepan over medium heat. Whisk in milk and cocoa, and bring mixture to a boil, whisking constantly. Remove from heat. Gradually add powdered sugar, stirring until smooth; stir in vanilla. Use immediately.

Note: To thin frosting, add 1 Tbsp. milk. To serve remaining Chocolate Frosting over pound cake or ice cream, microwave frosting in a medium-size microwave-safe glass bowl at HIGH 15 seconds or until warm.

½	cup butter
⅓	cup milk
¼	cup unsweetened cocoa
1	(16-oz.) package powdered sugar
1	tsp. vanilla extract

Coffee Liqueur-and-Cream Roulade

makes 8 servings
prep: 44 min. • cook: 18 min. • other: 1 hr., 30 min.

1 cup semisweet chocolate chunks
5 large eggs, separated
¾ cup granulated sugar
Parchment paper
3 Tbsp. unsweetened cocoa
1¼ cups whipping cream
3 Tbsp. powdered sugar
3 Tbsp. coffee liqueur
Garnishes: unsweetened cocoa, sifted powdered sugar, chocolate-covered coffee beans, whipped cream

tip:

• To test for doneness, gently jiggle the pan. If the cake is done, it will pull away from the sides of the pan when shaken.

• Be sure the damp towel directly touches the surface of the cake to keep the cake moist.

• To make ahead, prepare recipe as directed through Step 8. Place parchment paper-covered cake in freezer, cover securely with plastic wrap, and freeze up to 1 month. Transfer frozen cake to a serving platter, remove wrapping, and thaw in refrigerator 24 hours unwrapped. Garnish, if desired, just before serving.

1. Preheat oven to 325°. Microwave chocolate chunks and ¼ cup water in a large microwave-safe glass bowl at HIGH 1 minute or until chocolate chunks are melted, stirring at 30-second intervals.

2. Meanwhile, beat egg yolks and granulated sugar at high speed with an electric mixer, using whisk attachment, 2 to 3 minutes or until mixture is thick and pale yellow. Whisk into chocolate mixture.

3. Beat egg whites at high speed with an electric mixer until stiff peaks form. Fold one-third of egg whites into chocolate mixture; fold in remaining egg whites.

4. Line a lightly greased 15- x 10-inch jelly-roll pan with parchment paper. Lightly grease parchment paper. Pour batter into prepared pan.

5. Bake at 325° for 18 to 20 minutes or until puffed. Remove from oven, and cover surface of cake directly with a damp towel. Let cool 30 minutes or until completely cool.

6. Remove damp towel. Cut a 20- x 15-inch piece of parchment paper, and place on a cutting board or baking sheet. Dust cake with cocoa, and invert onto parchment paper. Carefully peel top layer of parchment paper from cake, and discard.

7. Beat whipping cream at low speed with electric mixer until foamy; add powdered sugar and coffee liqueur, and beat at high speed until stiff peaks form.

8. Spread cream mixture over top of cake, leaving a 1-inch border on all sides. Lift and tilt parchment paper at 1 short side, and roll up cake, jelly-roll fashion, using parchment paper as a guide. Wrap rolled cake in parchment paper, and place on a baking sheet.

9. Chill at least 1 hour or up to 8 hours. Transfer to a serving platter, seam side down; remove and discard parchment paper. Garnish, if desired.

Note: We tested with Kahlúa for coffee liqueur.

Remove kitchen towel from cooled cake, and dust cake surface with cocoa powder.

Invert cake onto a parchment paper-lined cutting board, and peel back top layer of parchment paper.

Spread cream mixture over surface of cake, and roll up, using parchment paper as a guide.

Heavenly Angel Food Cake

The rich, moist texture of this divine angel food cake is unlike any other. The two-step method for mixing the cake batter is unique, calling for a blend of sugar and flour to be folded into a billowy mound of egg whites.

makes 15 servings
prep: 15 min. • **cook: 30 min.** • **other: 1 hr.**

2 ½ cups sugar
1 ½ cups all-purpose flour
¼ tsp. salt
2 ½ cups egg whites
1 tsp. cream of tartar
1 tsp. vanilla extract
1 tsp. fresh lemon juice
Lemon-Cream Cheese Frosting
Garnishes: Gumdrop Rose Petals,
 fresh mint leaves

1. Preheat oven to 375°. Line bottom and sides of a 13- x 9-inch pan with aluminum foil, allowing 2 to 3 inches to extend over sides of pan. (Do not grease pan or foil.) Sift together first 3 ingredients.

2. Beat egg whites and cream of tartar at high speed with a heavy-duty electric stand mixer until stiff peaks form. Gradually fold in sugar mixture, ⅓ cup at a time, folding just until blended after each addition. Fold in vanilla and lemon juice. Spoon batter into prepared pan. (Pan will be very full. The batter will reach almost to the top of the pan.)

3. Bake at 375° on an oven rack one-third up from bottom of oven 30 to 35 minutes or until a wooden pick inserted in center of cake comes out clean. Invert cake onto a lightly greased wire rack; let cool, with pan over cake, 1 hour or until completely cool. Remove pan; peel foil off cake. Transfer cake to a serving platter. Spread Lemon-Cream Cheese Frosting evenly over top of cake. Garnish, if desired.

Lemon-Cream Cheese Frosting:

makes about 3½ cups
prep: 10 min.

1 ½ (8-oz.) packages cream cheese,
 softened
¼ cup butter, softened
¼ cup fresh lemon juice
1 (16-oz.) package powdered sugar
2 tsp. lemon zest

1. Beat cream cheese and butter at medium speed with an electric mixer until creamy; add lemon juice, beating just until blended. Gradually add powdered sugar, beating at low speed until blended; stir in lemon zest.

tip:

Two More Shapes for Cake. You may also bake this in an ungreased angel food cake pan for 30 to 35 minutes or in 3 ungreased 9-inch round pans for 15 to 18 minutes or until a wooden pick inserted in center comes out clean.

Gumdrop Rose Petals. You don't need a green thumb to make the candy rose petals that garnish Heavenly Angel Food Cake—just a handful of gumdrops and a dish of granulated sugar. Gumdrop flowers can be made weeks ahead and stored in an airtight container.

Use a single brightly colored gumdrop to shape the petals, or knead two colors together—such as red and white to make pink. Add more white to soften the color and create a paler pink, or add a pinch of yellow to highlight a portion of the petal. Experiment with different color combinations to see which you like best. For the prettiest petals, don't over-blend the colors or be too exact with the shaping. (Plan ahead when making rose petals: They need to stand for about 24 hours to stiffen slightly before adding the finishing touches that make them look so realistic.)

1. Dampen fingertips to prevent sticking when kneading gumdrops together. (A folded paper towel moistened with water works great—it's like a stamp pad for your fingertips.) It's easier to work with just 3 or 4 gumdrops at a time when blending new colors. After kneading several together, dredge lightly in sugar, and divide the mixture into small gumdrop-size portions for shaping individual petals and flowers.

2. Using your thumbs and forefingers, flatten 1 small gumdrop to ⅛-inch thickness, lengthening and widening to form a petal shape. Dredge lightly in granulated sugar to prevent sticking as you work. Repeat procedure for desired number of petals. Place petals on a wire rack, and let stand uncovered for 24 hours.

3. Holding each petal between your thumbs and forefingers, use your thumb to press the lower center portion of the petal inward, cupping the petal. Gently curl the top outer edges of the petal backward.

German Chocolate Snack Cake

makes 18 squares
prep: 15 min. • **cook: 1 hr., 5 min.** • **other: 1 hr.**

½ cup chopped pecans
1 (18.25-oz.) package German chocolate cake mix
4 large eggs, divided
½ cup butter, melted
1 (16-oz.) package powdered sugar
1 (8-oz.) package cream cheese, softened

1. Preheat oven to 350°. Arrange chopped pecans in a single layer in a shallow pan. Bake 5 to 7 minutes or until toasted and fragrant. Reduce oven temperature to 300°.

2. Stir together cake mix, 1 egg, butter, and toasted pecans; press mixture into bottom of a lightly greased 13- x 9-inch pan.

3. Beat sugar, cream cheese, and remaining 3 eggs at medium speed with an electric mixer until smooth. Pour powdered sugar mixture over batter in pan, spreading to edges.

4. Bake at 300° for 1 hour. Let cool 1 hour or until completely cool. Cut cake into 2½- to 3-inch squares.

Mocha Java Cakes

Even the cook will have a hard time believing these take less than 45 minutes to assemble and bake.

makes 6 servings
prep: 15 min. • **cook: 16 min.** • **other: 10 min.**

1. Preheat oven to 425°. Grease 6 (6-oz.) ramekins or individual soufflé dishes with 1 Tbsp. butter.

2. Microwave 1 cup butter and chocolate morsels in a microwave-safe bowl at HIGH 2 minutes or until chocolate is melted and mixture is smooth, whisking at 1-minute intervals.

3. Beat egg yolks and eggs at medium speed with an electric mixer 1 minute. Gradually add chocolate mixture, beating at low speed until well blended.

4. Sift together sugar and next 3 ingredients. Gradually whisk sugar mixture into chocolate mixture until well blended. Divide batter among prepared ramekins. Place ramekins in a 15- x 10-inch jelly-roll pan.

5. Bake at 425° for 16 minutes or until a thermometer inserted into cakes registers 165°. Remove from oven, and let stand 10 minutes. Run a knife around outer edge of each cake to loosen. Carefully invert cakes onto dessert plates. Garnish, if desired.

Note: We tested with Ghirardelli 60% Cacao Bittersweet Chocolate Chips.

chocolate decadence

1	Tbsp. butter
1	cup butter
8	oz. bittersweet chocolate morsels
4	egg yolks
4	large eggs
2	cups powdered sugar
¾	cup all-purpose flour
1	tsp. instant espresso or instant coffee granules

Pinch of salt
Garnish: powdered sugar

Petits fours, French for "small ovens," were originally prepared by bakers as a way to make use of the remaining heat in coal-fueled brick ovens as they cooled down at the end of a day of baking.

Chocolate-Almond Petits Fours

makes 3 dozen
prep: 45 min. • **cook: 8 min.** • **other: 1 hr., 3 min.**

Wax paper
¾   cup butter, softened
2   (8-oz.) cans almond paste
1½ cups sugar
8   large eggs
1½ cups all-purpose flour
1   (10-oz.) can apricot fruit spread
Chocolate Ganache (page 31)
Garnishes: almond slices, chopped
     dried apricots

1. Preheat oven to 400°. Grease bottom and sides of 2 (15- x 10-inch) jelly-roll pans, and line with wax paper; grease and flour wax paper.

2. Beat butter and almond paste at medium speed with an electric mixer until creamy. Gradually add sugar to butter mixture, beating well. Add eggs, 1 at a time, beating until blended after each addition. Stir in flour, and spread batter into prepared pans.

3. Bake at 400° for 8 to 10 minutes or until a wooden pick inserted in centers comes out clean. (Edges of cakes will just begin to brown.) Let cool in pans on wire racks 30 minutes.

4. Invert 1 cake onto a lightly floured, wax paper-lined surface; remove and discard top layer of wax paper. Spread apricot fruit spread over top of cake. Top with remaining cake; remove and discard top of wax paper. Cut out 36 cakes with a 1½-inch round cutter. Place cakes on a wire rack in a wax paper-lined large shallow pan.

5. Spoon Chocolate Ganache into a zip-top plastic freezer bag (do not seal). Snip 1 corner of bag to make a small (¼-inch) hole. Pipe a small amount of ganache onto tops and sides of cakes. Chill cakes 3 minutes. Pipe remaining ganache onto cakes, spreading with spatula to thoroughly cover cakes.

6. Chill petits fours at least 30 minutes or up to 24 hours. Store in an airtight container in freezer up to 3 months. Garnish, if desired.

Note: We tested with Polaner All Fruit Apricot Spread.

Baby Sweet Potato Cakes With Pecans and Sticky Caramel Sauce

makes 12 servings
prep: 25 min. • **cook: 23 min.** • **other: 5 min.**

1. Preheat oven to 350°. Beat softened butter and sugar at medium speed with an electric mixer until smooth. Add eggs, 1 at a time, beating until blended after each addition.

2. Combine flour and baking soda. Gradually add half of flour mixture to butter mixture, beating at low speed until blended. Add remaining half of flour mixture; beat until blended. Add vanilla and next 5 ingredients, beating at medium speed until smooth. Spoon batter into 12 muffin cups coated with cooking spray, filling two-thirds full.

3. Bake at 350° for 15 minutes or until a wooden pick inserted in center comes out clean. Let cool in pan on a wire rack 5 minutes.

4. Meanwhile, arrange pecans in a single layer in a shallow pan. Bake at 350° for 8 minutes or until toasted and fragrant.

5. Remove warm cakes from pan, and place upside down on serving plates, if desired. Sprinkle with toasted pecans. Top each cake with 2½ Tbsp. Sticky Caramel Sauce. Serve with vanilla ice cream or ice-cold heavy cream, if desired.

½	cup butter, softened
1	cup sugar
2	large eggs, at room temperature
1¼	cups all-purpose flour
1	tsp. baking soda
1	tsp. vanilla extract
½	tsp. salt
½	tsp. ground ginger
½	tsp. ground cinnamon
1	(15-oz.) can sweet potatoes, drained and mashed
⅓	cup buttermilk
	Vegetable cooking spray
½	cup chopped pecans
	Sticky Caramel Sauce
	Vanilla ice cream or heavy cream (optional)

Sticky Caramel Sauce:

makes about 2 cups
prep: 10 min. • **cook: 9 min.**

1. Cook brown sugar and butter in a medium nonstick skillet over medium heat 2 to 3 minutes or until sugar is dissolved and butter is melted. Whisk in heavy cream and coffee granules. Bring mixture to a light boil, stirring constantly. Turn off heat, and let stand on cooktop until slightly cool, stirring often.

¾	cup firmly packed light brown sugar
½	cup butter
1	cup heavy cream
½	tsp. instant coffee granules

Peanut Butter Surprise Cupcakes

You can use a coffee scoop, which equals about 2 tablespoons, to measure batter into paper baking cups.

makes 2 dozen
prep: 20 min. • **cook: 18 min.** • **other: 50 min.**

1. Preheat oven to 375°. Beat butter at medium speed with an electric mixer until creamy. Gradually add granulated sugar, beating until light and fluffy. Add eggs, 1 at a time, beating after each addition. Add peanut butter, beating until smooth.

2. Combine flour, baking soda, and salt; add to peanut butter mixture alternately with buttermilk, beginning and ending with flour mixture. Beat at low speed just until blended after each addition. Stir in vanilla.

3. Spoon 2 Tbsp. batter into each of 24 paper baking cups in muffin pans. Place 1 chocolate kiss on its side in center of batter in each cup. Top evenly with remaining batter (about 2 Tbsp. in each cup), covering chocolate kisses.

4. Bake at 375° for 18 to 20 minutes or until golden brown. Let cool in pans on wire racks 5 minutes. Remove from pans to wire racks, and cool completely (about 45 minutes). Dust with powdered sugar.

Peanut Butter-Jam Surprise Cupcakes: Prepare batter as directed. Spoon 2 Tbsp. batter into each of 24 paper baking cups in muffin pans. Omit milk chocolate kisses. Dollop 1 rounded tsp. of your favorite flavor jam in center of batter in each cup. Top evenly with remaining batter (about 2 Tbsp. in each cup). Bake and cool as directed.

kids love it

¾ cup butter, softened
2 cups granulated sugar
3 large eggs
1 cup creamy peanut butter
2 cups all-purpose flour
1 tsp. baking soda
½ tsp. salt
1 cup buttermilk
1 tsp. vanilla extract
24 paper baking cups
24 milk chocolate kisses
Powdered sugar

Chocolate-Peppermint Candy Cupcakes

makes 3 dozen
prep: 40 min. • **cook: 18 min.** • **other: 1 hr., 15 min.**

1. Preheat oven to 350°. Place 36 paper baking cups in muffin pans; spoon Chocolate Layer Cake batter evenly into baking cups, filling two-thirds full.

2. Bake at 350° for 18 minutes or until a wooden pick inserted in center comes out clean. Remove from pan to wire racks, and let cool 45 minutes or until completely cool.

3. Melt white chocolate morsels in a microwave-safe bowl at HIGH 1½ minutes or until melted and smooth, stirring at 30-second intervals. Spread melted chocolate in a ¼-inch-thick layer on an aluminum foil-lined baking sheet. Sprinkle with peppermint candy. Chill 30 minutes or until firm. Remove from baking sheet, and chop.

4. Spread cupcakes evenly with Vanilla Buttercream Frosting; sprinkle with chopped candy mixture.

tip:

Complete Cover Up. Spread frosting slightly over edge of cupcakes. Using back of spatula, gently smooth frosting to achieve a scalloped look.

kids love it

36 paper baking cups
Chocolate Layer Cake batter
    (page 24)
1   (12-oz.) package white chocolate
    morsels
½   cup crushed peppermint candy
    canes
Vanilla Buttercream Frosting
    (page 25)

Coconut Cupcakes

We call for using a mixer, but you can stir together by hand with great results. Because the mixer adds more air to the batter, you'll end up with 17 cakes rather than 24 when you stir them by hand.

makes 2 dozen
prep: 10 min. • **cook: 25 min.** • **other 1 hr., 10 min.**

1   (18.25-oz.) package white cake
       mix with pudding
1¼ cups buttermilk
¼   cup butter, melted
2   large eggs
2   tsp. vanilla extract
⅛   tsp. almond extract
Paper baking cups
Vegetable cooking spray
Coconut Buttercream
Garnish: sweetened flaked coconut

1. Preheat oven to 350°. Beat first 6 ingredients at low speed with an electric mixer just until dry ingredients are moistened. Increase speed to medium, and beat 2 minutes or until batter is smooth, stopping to scrape bowl as needed.

2. Place paper baking cups in muffin pans, and coat with cooking spray; spoon batter into baking cups, filling two-thirds full.

3. Bake at 350° for 25 minutes or until a wooden pick inserted in center comes out clean. Let cool in pans on wire racks 10 minutes. Remove from pans to wire racks, and let cool completely (about 1 hour). Spread with Coconut Buttercream, and, if desired, sprinkle with sweetened flaked coconut.

Note: We tested with Pillsbury Moist Supreme Classic White Cake Mix.

Coconut Buttercream:

makes 3 cups
prep: 10 min.

½   cup butter, softened
1   (3-oz.) package cream cheese
1   (16-oz.) package powdered sugar
¼   cup cream of coconut
1   tsp. vanilla extract

1. Beat butter and cream cheese at medium speed with an electric mixer until creamy. Gradually add powdered sugar, beating at low speed until blended. Increase speed to medium, and slowly add cream of coconut and vanilla, beating until smooth.

Crunchy Cookies & Chewy Bars

Stop here if you crave irresistibly delightful cookies that are sure to please any crowd. Chocolate, nuts, spices, and coffee beans are just a few of the choices you'll find in this chapter. Don't miss our Pecan Pie Cookies on page 123. They're so delicious, your guests will be asking for thirds!

From drop cookies to lemon bars and tea cakes to brownies, Southerners have a special affinity for the well-filled cookie jar.

Would you believe that cookies were first made by accident? Culinary historians agree that the very first cookies weren't cookies at all; they were actually just test cakes. Early cooks would bake a small amount of cake batter to test their oven temperatures before baking the real cake. These test cakes were called "koekje," the Dutch word for "little cake." And so we have the invention of the cookie. American cookbooks didn't distinguish these treats on their own at first; rather, cookie recipes were placed at the end of the cakes chapter. What a long way the cookie has come—nowadays, entire books are devoted to this favorite snack. Cookies come in an astonishing array of shapes and sizes, even without a cookie cutter at hand. Arguably the most popular variety of cookies today, drop cookies offer a quick fix to the occasional dilemma of "What can I serve? They'll be here in a couple of hours!" Ask your family, and you'll likely get a chorus of "chocolate chip," the classic American cookie.

In the South, classic sweets owe much of their lineage to plantation cooking and the fruits of the region. Whether it's a cookie filled with pecans, peanuts, or a splash of Kentucky Bourbon, one thing's for certain, so long as it's sweet, a Southerner will be happy.

Sand Dollar Cookies, Lemon Bars, and Pecan Pie Cookies are sure to satisfy any cookie-lover's craving for something sweet.

Chunky Chocolate-White Chocolate-Espresso Cookies

If you're looking for an amazingly good drop cookie, these thick cookies with soft white chocolate and a hint of coffee really hit the spot.

makes 15 cookies
prep: 14 min. • **cook: 21 min. per batch** • **other: 5 min.**

1. Preheat oven to 350°. Beat butter and sugar at medium speed with an electric mixer until blended. Add eggs and vanilla, beating just until blended. Microwave half of dark chocolate in a small, microwave-safe bowl at HIGH 50 seconds to 1 minute or until melted, stirring after 30 seconds. Add melted chocolate to butter mixture, beating just until blended.

2. Combine flour and next 3 ingredients; gradually add to butter mixture, beating just until blended after each addition. Stir in remaining dark chocolate, white chocolate, and pecans.

3. Drop dough by ⅓ cupfuls 2 inches apart onto lightly greased baking sheets.

4. Bake at 350° for 21 minutes. Let cool on baking sheets 5 minutes. Remove to wire racks, and cool completely.

Note: We tested with Ghirardelli Espresso Escape for dark chocolate bars and Ghirardelli for white chocolate bars.

¾ cup butter, softened
1½ cups sugar
2 large eggs
1 tsp. vanilla extract
2 (3.5-oz.) dark chocolate bars with finely ground espresso beans, chopped and divided
2¼ cups all-purpose flour
¼ cup cocoa
½ tsp. baking soda
¼ tsp. salt
2 (4-oz.) white chocolate bars, chopped
1 cup coarsely chopped pecan halves, toasted

In 1709, a toll house was built midway between Boston and New Bedford. Ruth Wakefield and her husband converted the toll house into an inn in 1930, and it became famous for its food. One day Mrs. Wakefield chopped up a chocolate bar and added it to a colonial cookie recipe, assuming it would melt. It didn't, but customers loved the cookies. In 1939, Nestlé introduced chocolate chips and, with Mrs. Wakefield's permission, put her recipe on the package. From that time forward, Mrs. Wakefield's "Toll House®" cookies have been universal favorites.

Ultimate Chocolate Chip Cookies

If you like soft and gooey cookies, bake them for the minimum time. If you prefer crispy ones, bake them longer.

makes about 5 dozen
prep: 30 min. • **cook: 10 min. per batch**

¾   cup butter, softened
¾   cup granulated sugar
¾   cup firmly packed dark brown sugar
2   large eggs
1½ tsp. vanilla extract
2 ¼ cups plus 2 Tbsp. all-purpose flour
1   tsp. baking soda
¾   tsp. salt
1   (12-oz.) package semisweet chocolate morsels

1. Preheat oven to 350°. Beat first 3 ingredients at medium speed with an electric mixer until creamy. Add eggs and vanilla, beating until blended.

2. Combine flour, baking soda, and salt in a small bowl; gradually add to butter mixture, beating well. Stir in morsels. Drop by tablespoonfuls onto parchment paper-lined baking sheets.

3. Bake at 350° for 10 to 14 minutes or to desired degree of doneness. Let cool on baking sheets 1 minute. Remove to wire racks, and cool completely. Store in airtight containers.

Pecan-Chocolate Chip Cookies: Preheat oven to 350°. Bake 1½ cups chopped pecans in a single layer in a shallow pan 8 to 10 minutes or until toasted and fragrant. Proceed with recipe as directed, stirring in toasted pecans with morsels.

Oatmeal-Raisin Chocolate Chip Cookies: Reduce flour to 2 cups. Proceed with recipe as directed, stirring 1 cup uncooked quick-cooking oats into dry ingredients in Step 2 and 1 cup raisins with morsels.

White Chocolate-Dipped Oatmeal-Cranberry Cookies

Dipping these cookies into white chocolate adds a dressed-up touch, but they're great plain, too.

makes about 4 dozen
prep: 46 min. • **cook: 9 min. per batch** • **other: 2 min.**

1	cup butter, softened
1	cup firmly packed light brown sugar
½	cup granulated sugar
1	large egg
1	Tbsp. vanilla extract
2	cups all-purpose flour
1	tsp. baking soda
½	tsp. baking powder
½	tsp. salt
2	cups sweetened dried cranberries
1 ½	cups pecan pieces, toasted
1 ¼	cups uncooked quick-cooking oats
3	(4-oz.) white chocolate baking bars, coarsely chopped
3	Tbsp. shortening

1. Preheat oven to 375°. Beat butter at medium speed with an electric mixer until creamy; gradually add sugars, beating well. Add egg and vanilla, beating until blended.

2. Combine flour and next 3 ingredients; gradually add to butter mixture, beating until blended. Stir in cranberries, pecans, and oats.

3. Drop dough by heaping tablespoonfuls 2 inches apart onto lightly greased baking sheets.

4. Bake at 375° for 9 to 11 minutes or until lightly browned. Let cool on baking sheets 2 minutes. Remove to wire racks, and cool completely.

5. Microwave white chocolate and shortening in a medium-size, microwave-safe bowl on HIGH 1 minute or until chocolate melts, stirring once. Dip half of each cookie into melted chocolate, letting excess drip back into bowl. Place dipped cookies on wax paper; let stand until firm.

Note: We tested with Craisins for dried cranberries and Ghirardelli for white chocolate baking bars.

tip:

To store cookie dough, use a small ice-cream scoop to shape dough into balls; place on a baking sheet, and freeze until firm. Transfer frozen balls to a zip-top plastic freezer bag. Remove as needed and bake frozen, allowing 2 to 3 minutes of extra baking time.

Most Southerners get excited about a few snowflakes in the sky, but the highest elevations of the Smoky Mountains of Tennessee and North Carolina get an average snowfall of 69 inches each winter. Reminiscent of the white-dusted mountain peaks, these cookies, with white chocolate and a dusting of powdered sugar, are as sweet as snowfall on a school day in the South.

Smoky Mountain Snowcaps

makes 3½ dozen
prep: 25 min. • **cook: 10 min. per batch**

1. Preheat oven to 350°. Melt white chocolate in a small saucepan over low heat, stirring until chocolate is smooth.

2. Beat butter and 1 cup sugar at medium speed with an electric mixer 5 minutes or until fluffy. Add eggs, 1 at a time, beating until blended after each addition. Add vanilla, beating well. Add melted chocolate, and beat 30 seconds.

3. Combine flour and next 3 ingredients; add to butter mixture, beating until blended. Stir in walnuts.

4. Drop dough by heaping tablespoonfuls onto lightly greased baking sheets.

5. Bake at 350° for 10 to 12 minutes or until edges are lightly browned. Remove to wire racks, and cool completely. Sprinkle with powdered sugar. Freeze up to 1 month in an airtight container, if desired.

6 oz. white chocolate, chopped
¾ cup butter, softened
1 cup granulated sugar
3 large eggs
1 tsp. vanilla extract
3½ cups all-purpose flour
1 tsp. baking powder
¾ tsp. salt
⅛ tsp. ground nutmeg
1½ cups chopped walnuts, toasted
½ cup powdered sugar

Soft Coconut Macaroons

makes about 3 dozen
prep: 10 min. • **cook: 18 min. per batch**

4   egg whites

2 ⅔ cups sweetened flaked coconut

⅔   cup sugar

¼   cup all-purpose flour or matzo
     meal

½   tsp. clear vanilla extract

¼   tsp. salt

¼   to ½ tsp. almond extract

1. Preheat oven to 325°. Stir together all ingredients in a large bowl, blending well. Drop dough by teaspoonfuls onto lightly greased baking sheets.

2. Bake at 325° for 18 to 20 minutes or until golden. Remove to wire racks to cool completely.

tip:

Using clear vanilla extract will keep the macaroons pearly white, but if you don't have it, regular vanilla extract will work fine.

Toffee-Oatmeal Cookies

makes 4 dozen
prep: 14 min. • **cook: 10 min. per batch**

½ cup butter, softened
½ cup firmly packed brown sugar
2 large eggs
1 tsp. vanilla extract
1½ cups uncooked regular oats
1 cup all-purpose flour
½ tsp. baking soda
¼ tsp. salt
½ cup chopped pecans
1½ cups (8 oz.) toffee bits

1. Preheat oven to 375°. Beat butter at medium speed with an electric mixer 2 to 3 minutes or until creamy. Add sugar, beating well. Add eggs and vanilla, beating until blended.

2. Combine oats and next 3 ingredients; add to butter mixture, beating just until blended. Stir in chopped pecans and toffee bits.

3. Drop dough by heaping tablespoonfuls onto lightly greased baking sheets.

4. Bake at 375° for 10 minutes. Remove to wire racks to cool completely.

Note: We tested with Hershey's Heath Bits O' Brickle Toffee Bits.

Lemon-Coconut Bars

makes 32 bars
prep: 10 min. • **cook: 56 min.** • **other: 30 min.**

1. Preheat oven to 350°. Place almonds in a single layer in a shallow pan. Bake at 350° for 6 to 8 minutes or until lightly toasted.

2. Combine flour and ½ cup powdered sugar. Cut butter into flour mixture with a pastry blender until crumbly; stir in almonds. Firmly press mixture into 2 lightly greased (9-inch-square) tart pans.

3. Bake at 350° for 20 to 25 minutes or until light golden brown.

4. Stir together Lemon Chess Pie Filling and coconut; pour over baked crust.

5. Bake at 350° for 30 to 35 minutes or until set. Let cool in pan on a wire rack 30 minutes. Sprinkle evenly with remaining ½ cup powdered sugar, and cut into bars.

½ cup chopped slivered almonds
2 cups all-purpose flour
1 cup powdered sugar, divided
1 cup butter, softened
Lemon Chess Pie Filling
1 cup sweetened flaked coconut

Lemon Chess Pie Filling:

makes about 3 cups
prep: 10 min.

1. Whisk together all ingredients. Use filling immediately.

2 cups sugar
4 large eggs
¼ cup butter, melted
¼ cup milk
1 Tbsp. lemon zest
¼ cup fresh lemon juice
1 Tbsp. all-purpose flour
1 Tbsp. cornmeal
¼ tsp. salt

Lemon Bars

We cut these bars into large servings for big lemon flavor.

makes 1 dozen
prep: 12 min. • **cook: 38 min.**

2 cups all-purpose flour
½ cup sifted powdered sugar
1 cup butter, softened
1 tsp. vanilla extract
2 cups granulated sugar
2 Tbsp. cornstarch
5 large eggs, lightly beaten
1 tsp. lemon zest
¼ cup plus 2 Tbsp. lemon juice
2 Tbsp. butter, melted
¼ cup powdered sugar

1. Preheat oven to 350°. Combine first 4 ingredients; beat at medium speed with an electric mixer until blended. Pat mixture into a greased 13- x 9-inch baking dish. Bake at 350° for 18 minutes or until golden.

2. Combine 2 cups granulated sugar and cornstarch. Add eggs and next 3 ingredients; beat well. Pour mixture over crust.

3. Bake at 350° for 20 to 25 minutes or until set. Let cool completely. Chill well.

4. Sift ¼ cup powdered sugar over top. Cut into bars.

Streusel-Topped Lemon Shortbread Bars

The thick shortbread crust and streusel topping set this recipe apart from all others.

makes 32 bars
prep: 15 min. • **cook: 1 hr., 1 min.**

1. Preheat oven to 350°. Combine first 3 ingredients in a food processor. Add ¾ cup butter to food processor, and pulse 12 to 15 times or until mixture resembles coarse meal. Add egg yolks to food processor, and process just until mixture forms clumps. (Clumps will be moist.) Press mixture onto bottom of a lightly greased 13- x 9-inch pan.

2. Bake at 350° for 16 to 18 minutes or just until edges are golden brown. Remove from oven, and reduce oven temperature to 325°.

3. Whisk together 6 eggs and 2 cups sugar in a large bowl until blended. Combine ½ cup flour and baking powder; whisk into egg mixture until blended. Whisk in lemon zest and lemon juice. Immediately pour lemon mixture over hot crust in pan.

4. Bake at 325° for 20 to 25 minutes or until filling is set. Remove from oven.

5. Combine ¼ tsp. salt and remaining ¾ cup flour and ½ cup sugar. Cut in ¼ cup butter pieces with a pastry blender or fork until crumbly. Sprinkle topping over hot lemon mixture.

6. Bake at 325° for 25 minutes or just until lightly golden. Let cool completely on a wire rack (about 1 hour). Cut into 32 bars, and sprinkle evenly with powdered sugar just before serving.

kids love it

2   cups all-purpose flour
3   Tbsp. granulated sugar
½   tsp. salt
¾   cup cold butter, cut into ½-inch pieces
2   egg yolks
6   large eggs
2 ½ cups granulated sugar, divided
1 ¼ cups all-purpose flour, divided
1   tsp. baking powder
4   tsp. lemon zest
½   cup fresh lemon juice
¼   tsp. salt
¼   cup cold butter, cut into ½-inch pieces
Powdered sugar

Cream Cheese Brownie Sundaes

kids love it

Top servings of this easy-to-make, yummy dessert with mint chocolate-chip ice cream and chocolate sauce for a cool treat.

makes 12 servings
prep: 20 min. • **cook: 35 min.**

1. Preheat oven to 350°. Beat cake mix, 1 egg, and butter at medium speed with an electric mixer until combined. Press mixture into the bottom of a lightly greased 13- x 9-inch baking dish.

2. Beat cream cheese and sugar at medium speed until smooth. Add remaining 2 eggs, 1 at a time, beating well after each addition. Gradually add cocoa, beating until blended. Pour mixture evenly over chocolate layer.

3. Bake at 350° for 35 to 40 minutes or until a wooden pick inserted in center comes out clean. Let cool completely. Cut into squares. Serve with mint chocolate-chip ice cream and chocolate sauce.

1   (18.25-oz.) box chocolate cake mix
3   large eggs, divided
½   cup butter, melted
1   (8-oz.) package cream cheese, softened
1   (16-oz.) box powdered sugar
⅓   cup unsweetened cocoa
Mint chocolate-chip ice cream
Chocolate sauce

Pecan Pie Brownies

Two popular sweets—rich chocolate brownies and Southern pecan pie—unite in this unique dessert. And thanks to a jump-start from frozen pie, it's ready for the oven with less than 30 minutes of hands-on prep time.

makes 40 small or 20 large brownies
prep: 25 min.   •   cook: 50 min.

1. Cut pie into cubes. Set aside.

2. Microwave butter and chocolate chunks in a microwave-safe bowl at HIGH 1 minute. Stir and microwave 1 more minute. Stir until mixture is smooth.

3. Preheat oven to 350°. Beat chocolate mixture, sugar, eggs, milk, and half of pie cubes at low speed with a heavy-duty electric stand mixer until blended.

4. Add flour and baking powder, stirring with a wooden spoon until blended. Stir remaining half of pie cubes into batter. (Batter will be thick.) Spoon batter into a 13- x 9-inch pan coated with cooking spray.

5. Bake at 350° for 50 minutes. Let cool completely on a wire rack. Cut into squares.

Note: We tested with Edwards Frozen Pecan Pie. Take the frozen pie out of the freezer 2 hours before you need to prepare this recipe so that it has time to thaw.

1	(2-lb.) frozen pecan pie, thawed (see Note)
½	cup butter
1 ¾	cups (11.5-oz. package) semi-sweet chocolate chunks
1	cup sugar
2	large eggs
1	cup milk
1 ½	cups all-purpose flour
1	tsp. baking powder

Cappuccino-Frosted Brownies

makes 10 to 12 servings
prep: 20 min. · **cook: 32½ min.** · **other: 1 hr.**

4   (1-oz.) unsweetened chocolate
     baking squares
¾   cup butter
2   cups sugar
4   large eggs
1   cup all-purpose flour
1   tsp. vanilla extract
1   cup semisweet chocolate
     morsels
Cappuccino Buttercream Frosting
Garnish: chocolate-covered espresso
     beans, chopped

1. Preheat oven to 350°. Microwave chocolate squares and butter in a large microwave-safe bowl at HIGH 2½ minutes or until melted and smooth, stirring at 30-second intervals. Stir in sugar. Add eggs, 1 at a time, beating with a spoon just until blended after each addition.

2. Stir in flour and vanilla until blended. Stir in chocolate morsels. Pour mixture into a lightly greased 13- x 9-inch pan.

3. Bake at 350° for 30 to 35 minutes or until a wooden pick inserted in center comes out clean. Let cool completely on a wire rack (about 1 hour).

4. Spread Cappuccino Buttercream Frosting on top of cooled brownies. Cut into squares. Garnish, if desired.

Cappuccino Buttercream Frosting:

makes 1½ cups
prep: 10 min. · **other: 15 min.**

1   (0.82-oz.) envelope 100-calorie
     café mocha cappuccino mix
¼   cup hot milk
½   cup butter, softened
1   (16-oz.) package powdered sugar
1   Tbsp. cold milk (optional)

1. Stir together cappuccino mix and hot milk in a small cup until mix is dissolved. Cover and chill until mixture cools completely (about 15 minutes).

2. Beat milk mixture and butter at medium speed with a heavy-duty electric stand mixer until well combined. Gradually add powdered sugar, beating until smooth and fluffy. Beat in 1 Tbsp. cold milk, if necessary, for desired consistency.

Note: We tested with General Foods International 100 Calorie Packs Café Mocha Cappuccino Mix.

tip:

When you beat the milk mixture and butter together, it may look curdled at first but will smooth out as you add the sugar.

Turtle Cookies

Georgia is the country's top producer of pecans, which come from the only major nut tree native to the U.S. In this recipe, milk chocolate morsels nestle between salty pecans for a candylike cookie.

makes 20 cookies
prep: 20 min. • **cook: 18 min.** • **other: 2 hr., 2 min.**

2	cups all-purpose flour
1	cup firmly packed brown sugar
½	cup butter, softened
1	cup pecan halves
⅔	cup butter
½	cup firmly packed brown sugar
1	cup milk chocolate morsels

1. Preheat oven to 350°. Combine first 3 ingredients in a mixing bowl; beat at medium speed with an electric mixer until blended. Pat mixture firmly into an ungreased 13- x 9-inch pan. Arrange pecans over crust.

2. Combine ⅔ cup butter and ½ cup brown sugar in a saucepan; bring to a boil over medium-high heat, stirring constantly. Cook 3 minutes, stirring constantly. Pour mixture over pecans. Bake at 350° for 15 to 17 minutes or until golden and bubbly.

3. Remove from oven; sprinkle with chocolate morsels. Let stand 2 to 3 minutes or until slightly melted. Gently swirl chocolate with a knife, leaving some morsels whole (do not spread). Let cool on a wire rack at room temperature until chocolate is set (about 2 hours). Cut into squares.

tip:
Arrange pecan halves in an even layer in Step 1 so that each cookie will have a pecan in it. Pecan halves make the prettiest cookies but chopped pecans taste just as delicious.

By the late 1800s in the South, locally made peanut butter was sold door to door in northeastern states. It wasn't until the 1920s that peanut butter was produced commercially.

Peanut Butter Squares

makes 2 dozen
prep: 15 min. • **other: 2 hr.**

4   cups sifted powdered sugar
1   (5 ⅓-oz.) package graham
     crackers, crushed (about
     1 ⅔ cups)
1   cup creamy peanut butter
1   cup butter, melted
1   cup semisweet chocolate
     morsels, melted

1. Stir together first 4 ingredients in a medium bowl. Firmly press mixture into an ungreased 13- x 9-inch pan. Spread melted chocolate evenly over cracker layer.

2. Let stand at room temperature 2 hours or until chocolate is set. Cut into squares.

Note: Layer Peanut Butter Squares between sheets of wax or parchment paper, and store in an airtight container up to 1 week, or freeze up to 1 month.

Chocolate Chip Cheesecake Bars

makes 12 bars
prep: 15 min. • **cook: 39 min.** • **other: 4 hr.**

1. Preheat oven to 350°. Beat first 3 ingredients at medium-low speed with an electric mixer until combined. Increase speed to medium, and beat until well blended and crumbly. Pat mixture into a lightly greased 13- x 9-inch pan. Bake at 350° for 13 to 15 minutes or until lightly browned.

2. Beat cream cheese at medium speed with an electric mixer until creamy. Gradually add granulated sugar, beating until well blended. Add eggs, 1 at a time, beating at low speed just until blended after each addition. Add sour cream, vanilla, and 1 cup chocolate morsels, beating just until blended. Pour over baked crust.

3. Bake at 350° for 25 minutes or until set. Let cool completely on a wire rack.

4. Microwave remaining chocolate morsels in a 2-cup glass measuring cup on HIGH 1 minute, stirring after 30 seconds. Stir until smooth. Let cool slightly. Drizzle over cheesecake. Cover and chill at least 4 hours; cut into bars.

chocolate decadence

1   cup all-purpose flour
⅓   cup firmly packed light brown
     sugar
¼   cup butter, softened
3   (8-oz.) packages cream cheese,
     softened
¾   cup granulated sugar
3   large eggs
⅓   cup sour cream
½   tsp. vanilla extract
1   (12-oz.) package chocolate mini-
     morsels, divided

tip:

To re-create the decorative look on top of the cheesecake bars, pour melted chocolate into a zip-top plastic freezer bag; close bag. Snip a tiny hole in a bottom corner of the bag to pipe melted chocolate onto the cheesecake bars.

Chocolate Cookie Bites

makes 2½ dozen
prep: 10 min. • **cook: 17 min.** • **other: 13 min.**

1. Preheat oven to 350°. Place pecans in a single layer in a shallow pan. Bake at 350° for 6 to 8 minutes or until lightly toasted, stirring once after 3 minutes.

2. Increase oven temperature to 400°. Beat 1 cup powdered sugar and butter at medium speed with an electric mixer until creamy. Add milk and vanilla, beating until blended.

3. Combine flour, cocoa, and salt; gradually add to butter mixture, beating until blended. Stir in pecans.

4. Shape dough into 1-inch balls, and place 1½ inches apart on lightly greased baking sheets.

5. Bake at 400° for 11 to 13 minutes or until tops of cookies just begin to crack. Let cool on baking sheets 3 minutes. Remove to wire racks; dust with remaining ¼ cup powdered sugar. Cool 10 minutes.

¾   cup chopped pecans
1¼   cups powdered sugar, divided
1   cup butter, softened
2   Tbsp. milk
1   tsp. vanilla extract
2   cups all-purpose flour
¼   cup unsweetened cocoa
¼   tsp. salt

Date Nugget Cookies

If you like chewy cookies, here's your recipe.
Dates, brown sugar, and walnuts make every bite
a taste of heaven.

makes 3 dozen
prep: 20 min. • **cook: 12 min. per batch**

1. Preheat oven to 350°. Beat shortening at medium speed with an electric mixer until fluffy; gradually add sugar, beating well. Add eggs; beat well.

2. Combine flour and next 3 ingredients; gradually add to shortening mixture, beating well. Stir in walnuts, dates, and vanilla. Shape dough into 1-inch balls; place 2 inches apart on greased baking sheets.

3. Bake at 350° for 12 minutes or until lightly browned. Let cool slightly on baking sheets. Remove to wire racks, and let cool completely.

1   cup shortening
1 ¼   cups firmly packed brown sugar
3   large eggs
2 ½   cups all-purpose flour
1   tsp. baking soda
½   tsp. salt
3   tsp. ground cinnamon
2   cups chopped walnuts
1 ½   cups chopped dates
1   tsp. vanilla extract

Oatmeal Cookie Sandwiches With Rum-Raisin Filling

A creamy rum-flavored filling glues these over-sized oatmeal cookies together for a rich treat that's a real handful.

makes 15 sandwiches
prep: 50 min. • **cook: 10 min. per batch** • **other: 23 min.**

½ cup butter, softened
½ cup shortening
¼ cup light corn syrup
1¼ cups firmly packed light brown sugar
1 large egg
1½ tsp. almond extract
1½ cups all-purpose flour
1 tsp. baking soda
1 tsp. ground cinnamon
½ tsp. salt
½ tsp. ground cloves
2 cups uncooked regular oats
¾ cup chopped pecans
Parchment paper
Rum-Raisin Filling

1. Preheat oven to 375°. Beat first 4 ingredients at medium speed with an electric mixer until fluffy. Add egg and almond extract, beating until blended.

2. Whisk together flour, baking soda, and next 3 ingredients in a medium bowl; gradually add to butter mixture, beating at low speed until blended after each addition. Stir in oats and pecans.

3. Shape dough into 1½-inch balls. Place balls 2 inches apart on large parchment paper-lined baking sheets.

4. Bake at 375° for 10 to 12 minutes or until golden. Let cool on baking sheets 3 minutes. Remove to wire racks, and cool completely (about 20 minutes). Spread about 3 Tbsp. Rum-Raisin Filling onto each of half the cookies; top with remaining cookies.

Rum-Raisin Filling:

makes 2½ cups
prep: 10 min.

1 (3-oz.) package cream cheese, softened
3 Tbsp. milk
1 Tbsp. dark rum*
¾ tsp. vanilla extract
⅛ tsp. salt
1 (1-lb.) package powdered sugar
1½ cups raisins

1. Beat cream cheese at medium speed with an electric mixer until creamy. Add milk and next 3 ingredients, beating until blended. Gradually add powdered sugar, beating at low speed until smooth. Stir in raisins.

*Omit rum, if desired.

Pecan Pie Cookies

bake & freeze

These nutty cookies keep the rich flavor of homemade pecan pie. Let your kids help shape and place the dough.

makes 4½ dozen
prep: 30 min. • **cook: 14 min.** • **other: 1 hr., 30 min.**

1. Beat 1 cup butter and sugar at medium speed with an electric mixer until light and fluffy. Add ½ cup corn syrup and egg yolks, beating well. Gradually stir in flour; cover and chill 1 hour.

2. Melt ¼ cup butter in a heavy saucepan over medium heat; stir in powdered sugar and 3 Tbsp. corn syrup. Cook, stirring often, until mixture boils. Remove from heat. Stir in pecans; chill 30 minutes. Shape mixture by ½ teaspoonfuls into ¼-inch balls; set aside.

3. Preheat oven to 375°. Shape cookie dough into 1-inch balls; place 2 inches apart on lightly greased baking sheets. Beat egg whites until foamy; brush on dough balls.

4. Bake at 375° for 6 minutes. Remove from oven, and place pecan balls in center of each cookie. Bake 8 to 10 more minutes or until lightly browned. Let cool 5 minutes on baking sheets. Remove to wire racks, and cool completely. Freeze up to 1 month, if desired.

1	cup butter, softened
½	cup sugar
½	cup dark corn syrup
2	large eggs, separated
2 ½	cups all-purpose flour
¼	cup butter
½	cup powdered sugar
3	Tbsp. dark corn syrup
¾	cup finely chopped pecans

In the early days of the South, the unique corn whiskey made in Kentucky was often referred to as Bourbon, the name of the county in which it was distilled. Today, it means the "good stuff"—or whiskey aged in charred oak barrels for at least two years. Hardly a Christmas can pass in the South without these traditional ball-shaped, bourbon-flavored pecan cookies ending up on a desserts table.

Bourbon Balls

makes 4 dozen
prep: 28 min.

1   (12-oz.) package vanilla wafers, finely crushed
1   cup chopped pecans or walnuts
¾   cup powdered sugar
2   Tbsp. cocoa
2 ½ Tbsp. light corn syrup
½   cup bourbon
Powdered sugar

1. Combine vanilla wafers, pecans, ¾ cup powdered sugar, and cocoa in a large bowl; stir well.

2. Combine corn syrup and bourbon; stirring well. Pour bourbon mixture over wafer mixture; stir until blended. Shape into 1-inch balls; roll in additional powdered sugar. Store in an airtight container up to 2 weeks.

kids love it

1 cup sugar
1 cup creamy peanut butter
1 large egg
1 tsp. vanilla extract

Easiest Peanut Butter Cookies

Easiest Peanut Butter Cookies are one of our favorites. The dough is easy to freeze so you can keep some on hand for whenever you need a quick snack.

makes about 2½ dozen
prep: 20 min. • cook: 15 min. per batch

1. Preheat oven to 325°. Stir together all ingredients in a large bowl until blended; shape dough into 1-inch balls. Place balls 1 inch apart on ungreased baking sheets, and flatten gently with tines of a fork.

2. Bake at 325° 15 minutes or until golden brown. Remove to wire racks, and cool completely.

Peanut Butter-and-Chocolate Cookies: Prepare dough as directed. Divide dough in half. Stir 2 melted semisweet chocolate baking squares into half of dough. Shape doughs into 30 (1-inch) balls, using half peanut butter and half chocolate-peanut butter dough for each ball. Proceed with recipe as directed, flattening dough balls gently with a spoon. Press 1 cup of your desired addition, such as chocolate morsels or chopped peanuts, onto the top of prepared cookie dough; bake as directed.

In Colonial days, when spices were hard to come by, Southern cooks made much use of fresh herbs, even for desserts such as pound cakes, sorbets, and cookies.

Lemon-Basil Butter Cookies

These sugar-sprinkled cookies with a trace of lemony-flavored basil are perfect for tea parties and special holiday gifts. Garnish a platter of them with fresh basil sprigs, unless you'd like to keep your guests guessing about the "secret" ingredient.

makes 6½ dozen

prep: 20 min. • **cook: 8 min. per batch**

1. Preheat oven to 350°. Process basil and ¼ cup sugar in a food processor until blended.

2. Beat butter at medium speed with an electric mixer until creamy; gradually add remaining 1½ cups sugar, beating well. Add lemon juice and egg, beating until blended. Gradually add flour and basil mixture, beating until blended.

3. Shape dough into 1-inch balls, and place 2 inches apart on lightly greased baking sheets. Flatten slightly with bottom of a glass dipped in sugar.

4. Bake at 350° for 8 to 10 minutes or until lightly browned. Remove to wire racks, and cool completely. Garnish, if desired.

*Plain fresh basil leaves may be substituted for lemon-basil leaves.

1	cup fresh lemon-basil leaves*
1¾	cups sugar, divided
1	lb. butter, softened
¼	cup lemon juice
1	large egg
6	cups all-purpose flour

Garnishes: fresh lemon-basil sprigs, lemon wedges

Some of the earliest mentions of this dainty dessert can be traced back to Savannah, Georgia. Katherine Keena, program manager at the Juliette Gordon Low birthplace in Savannah, reports: "In 1912, when Juliette Gordon Low was starting the Girl Scouts, she held many organizational teas where she was known for serving her 'little cakes.'"

Tea Cakes

makes 3 dozen
prep: 20 min. · **cook: 10 min. per batch** · **other: 1 hr., 5 min.**

1 cup butter, softened
2 cups sugar
3 large eggs
1 tsp. vanilla extract
3 ½ cups all-purpose flour
1 tsp. baking soda
½ tsp. salt
Parchment paper

1. Beat butter at medium speed with an electric mixer until creamy; gradually add sugar, beating well. Add eggs, 1 at a time, beating until blended after each addition. Add vanilla, beating until blended.

2. Combine flour, soda, and salt; gradually add flour mixture to butter mixture, beating at low speed until blended after each addition.

3. Divide dough in half; wrap each portion in plastic wrap, and chill 1 hour.

4. Preheat oven to 350°. Roll half of dough to ¼-inch thickness on a floured surface. Cut out cookies with a 2½-inch round cutter, and place 1 inch apart on parchment paper-lined baking sheets.

5. Bake at 350° for 10 to 12 minutes or until edges begin to brown; remove from oven and let stand on baking sheet 5 minutes. Remove to wire racks to cool completely. Repeat procedure with remaining dough.

tip:
For the best results, chill the tea cake dough thoroughly before you roll and cut it.

Sand Dollar Cookies

Package a few sand dollar cookies for an extra treat to give to dinner guests when they leave. In Louisiana that's called a "lagniappe," meaning a little something extra.

makes 4 dozen
prep: 25 min. · **cook: 14 min. per batch** · **other: 2 hr.**

1 cup butter, softened
2 cups sifted powdered sugar
2 large eggs
1 large egg, separated
3 ⅓ cups all-purpose flour
½ tsp. baking powder
Parchment paper
¼ cup granulated sugar
1 tsp. ground cinnamon
Sliced almonds

1. Beat butter at medium speed with an electric mixer until creamy; gradually add 2 cups sifted powdered sugar, beating until well blended. Add 2 eggs and 1 egg yolk, beating until blended.

2. Combine flour and baking powder. Add to butter mixture, beating at low speed until blended. Shape dough into a ball, and wrap in plastic wrap. Chill 2 hours.

3. Preheat oven to 350°. Roll dough to ⅛-inch thickness on a lightly floured surface; cut with a 3-inch round cutter. Place on lightly greased, parchment paper-lined baking sheets; brush with lightly beaten egg white.

4. Stir together granulated sugar and ground cinnamon, and sprinkle evenly over cookies. Gently press 5 almond slices in a spoke design around center of each cookie.

5. Bake at 350° for 4 minutes; remove pan from oven, and gently press almonds into cookies again. Bake 10 more minutes or until edges are lightly browned. Remove cookies to wire racks, and cool completely.

tip:

To get ahead, chill the dough up to 3 days in advance. Before rolling, let it stand at room temperature about 30 minutes to soften.

Classic Sugar Cookies

Cut this dough into a variety of your favorite shapes. The dippable glaze will transform the cookies into works of art almost too pretty to eat.

makes 20 cookies
prep: 25 min. · **cook: 8 min. per batch** · **other: 1 hr.**

1. Preheat oven to 350°. Beat butter at medium speed with an electric mixer until creamy. Gradually add granulated sugar, beating well. Add egg and vanilla, beating well. Combine flour and salt. Gradually add to butter mixture, beating until blended. Divide dough in half. Cover and chill 1 hour.

2. Roll each portion of dough to ¼-inch thickness on a lightly floured surface. Cut with desired cookie cutters. (We used flower and starfish cutters.) Place on lightly greased baking sheets.

3. Bake at 350° for 8 to 10 minutes or until edges of cookies are lightly browned. Let cool on baking sheets 1 minute. Remove to wire rack, and cool completely.

4. Dip cookies in Sugar Cookie Glaze and sprinkle, while wet, with sparkling sugar.

1	cup butter, softened
1	cup granulated sugar
1	large egg
1	tsp. vanilla extract
3	cups all-purpose flour
¼	tsp. salt
	Sugar Cookie Glaze
1	(3.25-oz.) jar coarse sparkling sugar

Sugar Cookie Glaze:

makes 1⅓ cups
prep: 5 min.

1. Stir together powdered sugar and warm water using a wire whisk. Divide mixture, and tint with food coloring, if desired; place in shallow bowls for ease in dipping cookies.

1	(16-oz.) package powdered sugar
6	Tbsp. warm water
	Liquid food coloring (optional)

tip:

For the cleanest cookie cutouts, when making an impression with a cookie cutter, cut straight down into the dough— don't twist. Best results come when you're working with a firm or chilled dough that's just been rolled.

How can a few simple ingredients come together to make a treat as good as shortbread? As generations of Scots can attest, that magic triplicity of butter, sugar, and flour can even make a nation proud.

Browned Butter-Pecan Shortbread

Buttery shortbread cookies are so tender they melt in your mouth. Toasted pecans and butter cooked until browned add a warm, cozy flavor that calls for a cup of hot tea or coffee and a few minutes to savor every bite.

makes about 10½ dozen
prep: 30 min. • cook: 6 min., plus 8 min. per batch • other: 5 hr.

1½ cups butter, cut into pieces
¾ cup firmly packed brown sugar
¾ cup powdered sugar
3 cups all-purpose flour
1½ cups finely chopped toasted pecans

1. Cook butter in a large skillet over medium heat, stirring constantly, 6 to 8 minutes or until butter begins to turn golden brown. Remove pan from heat immediately, and pour butter into a shallow dish. Do not cover. Chill 1 hour or until butter is cool and begins to solidify.

2. Beat butter at medium speed with an electric mixer until creamy. Gradually add sugars, beating until smooth. Gradually add flour to butter mixture, beating at low speed just until blended. Stir in pecans.

3. Shape dough into 4 (8-inch) logs. Wrap logs tightly in plastic wrap, and chill 4 hours or until firm.

4. Preheat oven to 350°. Cut logs into ¼-inch-thick rounds; place on lightly greased baking sheets. Bake at 350° for 8 to 10 minutes or until lightly browned. Remove to wire racks, and let cool completely.

Note: Finely chopping the pecans makes the logs easier to cut in Step 4.

Jam Kolache

Four-ingredient gems with a flavorful burst of strawberry jam tucked inside, these little treats are the big attraction at the annual Kolache Festival. This Caldwell, Texas, event is more than 20 years old and is hosted by proud descendents of early Czechoslovakian immigrants to Central Texas.

makes 3½ dozen
prep: 16 min. • **cook: 15 min. per batch**

½ cup butter, softened
1 (3-oz.) package cream cheese, softened
1 ¼ cups all-purpose flour
Strawberry jam (about ½ cup)

1. Preheat oven to 375°. Beat butter and cream cheese at medium speed with an electric mixer until creamy. Add flour to butter mixture, beating well.

2. Roll dough to ⅛-inch thickness on a lightly floured surface; cut with a 2½-inch round cookie cutter. Place on lightly greased cookie sheets. Spoon ¼ tsp. jam on each cookie. Fold opposite sides to center, slightly overlapping edges; press down lightly on centers.

3. Bake at 375° for 15 minutes. Remove to wire racks, and cool completely.

Cocoa-Almond Biscotti

Biscotti are intensely crunchy Italian cookies, perfect for dunking into a cup of hot coffee. Enjoy them for breakfast or dessert.

makes 2 dozen
prep: 20 min. • **cook: 38 min.**

1. Preheat oven to 350°. Beat butter and sugar in a large bowl at medium speed with an electric mixer until creamy. Add eggs, beating well. Mix in liqueur.

2. Combine flour and next 3 ingredients; add to butter mixture, beating at low speed until blended. Stir in almonds.

3. Divide dough in half; using floured hands, shape each portion into a 9- x 2-inch log on a lightly greased cookie sheet.

4. Bake at 350° for 28 to 30 minutes or until firm. Let cool on cookie sheet 5 minutes. Remove to a wire rack, and let cool completely.

5. Cut each log diagonally into ¾-inch-thick slices with a serrated knife, using a gentle sawing motion. Place slices on ungreased baking sheets. Bake 5 minutes. Turn cookies over, and bake 5 to 6 more minutes. Remove to wire racks, and cool completely.

½	cup butter, softened
1	cup sugar
2	large eggs
1½	Tbsp. Kahlúa or other coffee-flavored liqueur
2½	cups all-purpose flour
1½	tsp. baking powder
¼	tsp. salt
3	Tbsp. Dutch process cocoa or regular unsweetened cocoa
1	(6-oz.) can whole almonds

S'more Puffs

These s'mores are as simple to make as they look. Once they bake, stack a few to create a pretty presentation.

makes 12 puffs
prep: 5 min. • **cook: 8 min.** • **other: 5 min.**

1. Preheat oven to 350°. Place crackers on a baking sheet. Top each with 1 milk chocolate kiss and 1 marshmallow half, cut side down. Bake 8 minutes or just until marshmallows begin to melt. Let cool on a wire rack 5 minutes.

12   round buttery crackers
12   milk chocolate kisses
6   large marshmallows, cut in half

tip:

Line the baking sheet with aluminum foil for easy cleanup. Keep in mind that the center of the marshmallow will still be warm after the cooling time. Chocolate kisses will soften but not melt.

kids love it

Cheesecakes to Die For

Create a lasting impression for a loved one with a smooth and creamy cheesecake. Whether you prefer the rich decadence of chocolate or the sweet taste of fresh fruit, we have the perfect choice for you. We even offer a lightened version that's so good you won't miss the calories. What a great way to end a meal.

Classic Southern

The South can't take responsibility for inventing the cheesecake, but we sure can enjoy it. Traditional and novel cheesecakes alike, Southerners can't get enough of this decadent dessert.

Believe it or not, cheesecake didn't get its beginning in New York or Philadelphia. History tells us that this favorite dessert dates back to the ancient Greeks, who served small cheesecakes to athletes at the first Olympic Games in 776 B.C. After the Roman conquest of ancient Greece, cheesecake slowly spread across the continent and finally made its way to America with the arrival of European immigrants. The cheesecake recipes of today are likely different from the ones used centuries ago. Before cream cheese existed, Neufchâtel, a soft, unripened French cheese, was a popular choice for making the dessert. The discovery of cream cheese was a mistake, in fact—in 1872, American dairyman William Lawrence of

Chester, New York was attempting to make Neufchâtel when he accidentally invented cream cheese, a richer version of the French cheese. Then, in 1912, James Kraft developed pasteurized cream cheese, which we now know as Philadelphia Cream Cheese. The Philadelphia brand is perhaps the most familiar name in making cheesecake today. All preferences aside, one thing's for sure: Modern-day cheesecake simply wouldn't be cheesecake without that perfectly rich brick of cream cheese.

Rich, smooth cheesecake is a great dessert choice because it can be made ahead and chilled. Chocolate Fudge Cheesecake, Uptown Banana Pudding Cheesecake, and Free-form Strawberry Cheesecake are elegant options.

New York-Style Sour Cream-Topped Cheesecake

makes 16 servings
prep: 20 min. • **cook: 50 min.** • **other: 4 hr., 30 min.**

1. Preheat oven to 325°. Line bottom and sides of a 13- x 9-inch pan with aluminum foil, allowing 2 to 3 inches to extend over sides. Stir together cracker crumbs, butter, and 2 Tbsp. sugar; press firmly onto bottom of prepared pan.

2. Beat cream cheese, 1 cup sugar, and 1 tsp. vanilla at medium speed with an electric mixer until well blended. Add 1 cup sour cream, beating well. Add eggs, 1 at a time, beating at low speed just until blended after each addition. Pour over crust.

3. Bake at 325° for 40 minutes or until center is almost set. Stir together remaining sour cream, 2 Tbsp. sugar, and 1 tsp. vanilla until well blended; carefully spread over cheesecake.

4. Bake 10 more minutes. Let cool on a wire rack 30 minutes. Cover and chill at least 4 hours or up to 24 hours. Lift cheesecake from pan, using foil sides as handles. Top with strawberries just before serving. Store leftover cheesecake in refrigerator.

New York-Style Cinnamon Cheesecake: Stir together cracker crumbs, butter, and sugar as directed in Step 1. Press mixture onto bottom and 1 inch up sides of a lightly greased 9-inch springform pan. Prepare batter as directed in Step 2, beating in 1½ tsp. ground cinnamon with cream cheese. Bake at 325° for 50 minutes or until center is almost set. Top with sour cream mixture as directed, and bake 10 more minutes. Remove from oven, and gently run a knife around the edges of cheesecake to loosen. Let cool and chill as directed. Omit strawberries. Garnish with sliced almonds, fresh rosemary sprigs, and pear slices, if desired.

1½ cups graham cracker crumbs
¼   cup butter, melted
1¼ cups sugar, divided
4   (8-oz.) packages cream cheese, softened
2   tsp. vanilla extract, divided
1   (16-oz.) container sour cream, divided
4   large eggs
2   cups sliced fresh strawberries

Irish Strawberry-and-Cream Cheesecake

makes 10 to 12 servings
prep: 20 min. • **cook: 1 hr., 5 min.** • **other: 8 hr., 15 min.**

1. Preheat oven to 325°. Stir together first 3 ingredients; press mixture into bottom of a lightly greased 9-inch springform pan. Bake crust at 325° for 10 minutes. Let cool on a wire rack. Reduce oven temperature to 300°.

2. Beat cream cheese, 1 cup sugar, and 3 Tbsp. flour at medium speed with an electric mixer until smooth. Gradually add vanilla and Irish cream liqueur, beating just until blended. Add eggs, 1 at a time, beating at low speed just until blended after each addition. Add ¾ cup sour cream, beating just until blended.

3. Pour half of batter into prepared crust. Dollop strawberry preserves over batter; gently swirl batter with a knife to create a marbled effect. Top with remaining batter.

4. Bake at 300° for 55 minutes or until edges of cheesecake are set. (Center of cheesecake will not appear set.) Turn oven off; let cheesecake stand in oven 15 minutes. Remove cheesecake from oven; gently run a knife around edge of cheesecake to loosen. Let cool completely on a wire rack. Cover and chill 8 hours.

5. Release and remove sides of pan. Spread remaining ½ cup sour cream over top of cheesecake; garnish, if desired.

Note: We tested with Baileys Irish Cream.

1	cup graham cracker crumbs
3	Tbsp. butter, melted
3	Tbsp. sugar
4	(8-oz.) packages cream cheese, softened
1	cup sugar
3	Tbsp. all-purpose flour
2	tsp. vanilla extract
¼	cup Irish cream liqueur
4	large eggs
1¼	cups sour cream, divided
3	Tbsp. strawberry preserves
Garnish: whole strawberries	

Chocolate Fudge Cheesecake

makes 20 servings
prep: 30 min. • **cook: 1 hr., 4 min.** • **other: 9 hr.**

1. Preheat oven to 350°. Arrange chopped pecans in a single layer in a shallow pan. Bake at 350° for 4 to 6 minutes or until toasted and fragrant. Reduce oven temperature to 325°.

2. Sprinkle toasted pecans over bottoms of 2 greased and floured 9-inch springform pans.

3. Microwave chocolate baking squares in a microwave-safe bowl at MEDIUM (50% power) 1½ minutes or until melted and smooth, stirring at 30-second intervals.

4. Beat butter and 2 cups sugar at medium speed with an electric mixer until light and fluffy. Add 4 eggs, 1 at a time, beating just until blended after each addition. Add melted chocolate, beating just until blended. Add flour, beating at low speed just until blended. Stir in chocolate morsels and 1 tsp. vanilla. Divide batter between pans, spreading to edges of pan over chopped pecans.

5. Beat cream cheese at medium speed until smooth; add remaining 1¾ cups sugar, beating until blended. Add remaining 7 eggs, 1 at a time, beating just until blended after each addition. Stir in remaining 2 tsp. vanilla. Divide cream cheese mixture between pans, spreading over chocolate batter.

6. Bake at 325° for 1 hour or until set. Remove from oven; gently run a knife around edges of cheesecakes to loosen. Let cool completely on wire racks (about 1 hour).

7. Spread tops of cooled cheesecakes with Chocolate Glaze; cover and chill 8 hours. Remove sides of pans. Garnish, if desired.

½	cup finely chopped pecans
4	(1-oz.) unsweetened chocolate baking squares
1	cup butter, softened
3 ¾	cups sugar, divided
11	large eggs, divided
1	cup all-purpose flour
1	cup semisweet chocolate morsels
3	tsp. vanilla extract, divided
4	(8-oz.) packages cream cheese, softened

Chocolate Glaze
Garnish: chocolate-dipped pecan halves

Chocolate Glaze:

makes 2 cups
prep: 5 min.

1. Melt semisweet chocolate morsels and whipping cream in a 2-qt. microwave-safe bowl at MEDIUM (50% power) 2½ to 3 minutes or until chocolate begins to melt, stirring at 1-minute intervals. Whisk until chocolate melts and mixture is smooth.

1	(12-oz.) package semisweet chocolate morsels
½	cup whipping cream

Lightened Chocolate-Coffee Cheesecake With Mocha Sauce

makes 10 servings
prep: 20 min. • **cook: 1 hr., 10 min.** • **other: 5 hr., 30 min.**

2   cups crushed chocolate graham crackers (about 18 crackers) (see Note)
⅓   cup light butter, melted
Vegetable cooking spray
4   (8-oz.) packages ⅓-less-fat cream cheese, softened
1   cup sugar
¼   cup coffee liqueur
1   tsp. vanilla extract
1   tsp. instant coffee granules
4   large eggs
4   (1-oz.) bittersweet chocolate baking squares
Mocha Sauce

1. Preheat oven to 350°. Stir together crushed graham crackers and melted butter; press mixture into bottom and up sides of a 9-inch springform pan coated with cooking spray. Bake at 350° for 10 minutes. Let cool on a wire rack. Reduce oven temperature to 325°.

2. Meanwhile, beat cream cheese and sugar at medium speed with an electric mixer until blended. Add liqueur, vanilla, and coffee granules, beating at low speed until well blended. Add eggs, 1 at a time, beating just until yellow disappears after each addition.

3. Reserve 1 cup cream cheese batter. Pour remaining batter into prepared crust.

4. Microwave chocolate in a medium-size, microwave-safe bowl at HIGH 1 minute or until melted, stirring after 30 seconds. Stir reserved 1 cup cream cheese mixture into melted chocolate, blending well. (Mixture will be thick.) Dollop chocolate mixture on top of batter in pan; gently swirl with a knife.

5. Bake at 325° for 1 hour or until almost set. Turn oven off. Let cheesecake stand in oven, with door closed, 30 minutes. Remove cheesecake from oven, and gently run a knife around edge of cheesecake to loosen. Let cool in pan on a wire rack 1 hour. Cover and chill at least 4 hours or up to 24 hours.

6. Remove sides of pan. Serve cheesecake with Mocha Sauce.

Note: We tested with Nabisco Chocolate Teddy Grahams Graham Snacks and Kahlúa.

Mocha Sauce:

makes ¾ cup
prep: 10 min. • **cook: 2 min.**

1   cup semisweet chocolate morsels
¼   cup half-and-half
2   tsp. light butter
3   Tbsp. strong-brewed coffee

1. Cook first 3 ingredients in a small heavy saucepan over low heat, stirring often, 2 to 3 minutes or until smooth. Remove from heat, and stir in coffee. Serve warm.

Reserve 1 cup cream cheese batter. Pour remaining batter into prepared crust.

Stir reserved cream cheese batter into melted chocolate.

Dollop chocolate mixture over batter, and swirl gently with a knife.

Double Chocolate Cheesecake

chocolate decadence

The sweetness of this cheesecake checks in at just the right level to let the chocolate flavor stand out.

makes 8 to 10 servings
prep: 20 min. • **cook: 1 hr., 5 min.** • **other: 9 hr., 30 min.**

1. Preheat oven to 300°. Place cookies in a zip-top plastic freezer bag; crush with a rolling pin. (Crumbs should equal about 1½ cups). Press cookie crumbs on bottom and halfway up sides of a 9-inch springform pan.

2. Microwave chocolate morsels in a microwave-safe bowl at HIGH 1½ minutes or until melted, stirring at 30-second intervals.

3. Beat cream cheese at medium speed with an electric mixer 2 minutes or until smooth. Add sweetened condensed milk and vanilla, beating at low speed just until combined. Add eggs, 1 at a time, beating at low speed just until combined after each addition. Add melted chocolate, beating just until combined. Pour cheesecake batter into prepared crust.

4. Bake at 300° for 1 hour and 5 minutes or just until center is set. Turn oven off. Let cheesecake stand in oven, with door closed, 30 minutes. Remove cheesecake from oven; run a knife along edge of cheesecake to loosen, and let cool in pan on a wire rack until room temperature. Cover and chill 8 hours.

5. Remove sides of pan, and place cake on a serving plate. Slowly pour and spread warm Ganache Topping over top of cheesecake, letting it run down sides of cheesecake. Cover and chill 1 hour before serving.

18	to 20 cream-filled chocolate sandwich cookies
1	(12-oz.) package semisweet chocolate morsels
3	(8-oz.) packages cream cheese, softened
1	(14-oz.) can sweetened condensed milk
2	tsp. vanilla extract
4	large eggs
	Ganache Topping

Ganache Topping:

makes 1½ cups
prep: 10 min. • **cook: 3 min.** • **other: 30 min.**

1. Bring cream to a boil in a saucepan over medium heat; quickly remove from heat, and stir in semisweet and milk chocolate morsels until melted and smooth. Let mixture cool (about 30 minutes) until slightly warm; pour and spread over cheesecake.

¾	cup whipping cream
1	(6-oz.) package semisweet chocolate morsels (1 cup)
1	(6-oz.) package milk chocolate morsels (1 cup)

Uptown Banana Pudding Cheesecake

makes 10 to 12 servings
prep: 25 min. • **cook: 56 min.** • **other: 8 hr.**

1. Preheat oven to 350°. Combine first 3 ingredients in a small bowl. Press into bottom of a greased 9-inch springform pan. Bake at 350° for 10 minutes. Let cool on a wire rack.

2. Combine diced bananas and lemon juice in a small saucepan. Stir in brown sugar. Place over medium-high heat, and cook, stirring constantly, about 1 minute or just until sugar melts. Set banana mixture aside.

3. Beat cream cheese at medium speed with an electric mixer 3 minutes or until smooth. Gradually add granulated sugar, beating until blended. Add eggs, 1 at a time, beating until blended after each addition. Beat in liqueur and vanilla. Pour into prepared pan. Spoon tablespoonfuls of banana mixture evenly over top, and swirl gently into batter.

4. Bake at 350° for 35 to 40 minutes or until center is almost set. Remove from oven, and increase oven temperature to 400°.

5. Drop spoonfuls of Meringue gently and evenly over hot cheesecake. Bake at 400° for 10 minutes or until Meringue is golden brown. Remove from oven, and gently run a knife around edge of cheesecake to loosen. Cool cheesecake completely in pan on a wire rack. Cover loosely, and chill 8 hours. Store in refrigerator.

1½	cups finely crushed vanilla wafers
¼	cup chopped walnuts, toasted
¼	cup butter, melted
2	large ripe bananas, diced
1	Tbsp. lemon juice
2	Tbsp. light brown sugar
3	(8-oz.) packages cream cheese, softened
1	cup granulated sugar
3	large eggs
1	Tbsp. coffee liqueur
2	tsp. vanilla extract
	Meringue

Meringue:

makes about 2 cups
prep: 11 min.

1. Beat egg whites and salt at high speed with an electric mixer until foamy. Add sugar, 1 Tbsp. at a time, beating until soft peaks form and sugar dissolves (about 1 to 2 minutes).

3	egg whites
¼	tsp. salt
6	Tbsp. sugar

Praline-Crusted Cheesecake

makes 12 servings
prep: 30 min. • **cook: 68 min.** • **other: 9 hr., 15 min.**

1½ (7-oz.) packages pure butter shortbread rounds with sugared edges

3 Tbsp. butter, melted

4 Pralines, coarsely crumbled

5 (8-oz.) packages cream cheese, softened

1¾ cups sugar

2 Tbsp. all-purpose flour

1½ tsp. vanilla extract

4 large eggs

2 egg yolks

⅓ cup whipping cream

1 tsp. lemon zest

2 (8-oz.) containers sour cream

⅓ cup sugar

Garnish: crumbled Pralines

1. Preheat oven to 350°. Process shortbread in a blender or food processor 15 to 20 seconds or until graham cracker crumb consistency. Combine shortbread crumbs and butter. Press into bottom and up sides of a greased aluminum foil-lined 10-inch springform pan. Bake at 350° for 8 minutes. Let cool on a wire rack 15 minutes. Sprinkle Pralines over crust.

2. Beat cream cheese at medium speed with a heavy-duty electric mixer until creamy. Gradually add 1¾ cups sugar, 2 Tbsp. flour, and 1½ tsp. vanilla, beating until smooth. Add eggs and egg yolks, 1 at a time, beating just until yellow disappears. Stir in whipping cream and lemon zest. Pour into prepared crust. Place on an aluminum foil-lined baking sheet.

3. Bake at 350° on lower oven rack 10 minutes. Reduce oven temperature to 325°, and bake 40 to 45 minutes or until almost set. Turn oven off. Let stand in oven, with door partially open, 1 hour.

4. Stir together sour cream and ⅓ cup sugar; spread mixture over cheesecake.

5. Bake at 325° on middle oven rack 10 minutes. Let cool completely on a wire rack (about 30 minutes). Cover and chill 8 hours. Gently run a knife around edge of cheesecake to loosen. Remove sides of pan. Garnish, if desired.

Note: We tested with Walkers Pure Butter Shortbread Highlanders.

Pralines:

makes 1 dozen
prep: 25 min. • **cook: 10 min.** • **other: 33 min.**

1. Butter bottom of a heavy 3-qt. saucepan with 1 Tbsp. butter. Cook brown sugar and next 3 ingredients in buttered saucepan over low heat, stirring constantly, 4 to 6 minutes or until sugars are dissolved and butter is melted. Stir in pecans. Bring to a boil over medium heat; cook, stirring occasionally, until a candy thermometer registers 238° (soft-ball stage, about 6 to 8 minutes). Remove from heat.

2. Stir in vanilla, and let stand 3 minutes. Beat mixture by hand with a wooden spoon 3 minutes or until mixture begins to thicken. Working rapidly, drop by tablespoonfuls onto wax paper. Let stand 30 minutes or until firm.

1	Tbsp. butter
¾	cup firmly packed light brown sugar
¾	cup granulated sugar
¾	cup half-and-half
3	Tbsp. butter
1 ¼	cups coarsely chopped pecans
¼	tsp. vanilla extract

Blueberry Mini Cheesecakes

makes 10 servings
prep: 30 min. • **cook: 53 min.** • **other: 9 hr., 15 min.**

1. Preheat oven to 350°. Place almonds in a single layer in a shallow pan. Bake 10 minutes or until lightly toasted and fragrant, stirring after 5 minutes. Let cool 15 minutes or until completely cool.

2. Pulse almonds in a food processor 5 to 6 times or until finely ground. Combine ground almonds, ¼ cup sugar, 3 Tbsp. butter, and 1 Tbsp. flour in a small bowl. Press mixture onto bottom and halfway up sides of 5 lightly greased 4½-inch springform pans.

3. Bake crusts at 350° for 8 minutes. Let cool on a wire rack. Reduce oven temperature to 300°.

4. Beat cream cheese at medium speed with an electric mixer until smooth. Combine remaining 1¼ cups sugar, remaining 3 Tbsp. flour, and ½ tsp. salt. Add to cream cheese, beating until blended. Add eggs, 1 at a time, beating well after each addition. Add 1 (8-oz.) container sour cream, vanilla, and lemon zest, beating just until blended. Gently stir in blueberries. Spoon about 1½ cups batter into each prepared crust. (Pans will be almost full. Batter will reach about ¼ inch from tops of pans.) Place on a baking sheet.

5. Bake at 300° for 35 to 40 minutes or until center is firm. Turn oven off. Let stand in oven, with door partially open, 30 minutes.

6. Remove cheesecakes from oven; gently run a knife around edges of cheesecakes to loosen. Let cool completely on a wire rack (about 30 minutes). Cover and chill 8 hours. Release sides of pans.

7. Beat whipping cream at high speed until foamy; gradually add 2 tsp. sugar, beating until stiff peaks form. Fold in 2 Tbsp. sour cream. Spread over cheesecake, and garnish, if desired.

Note: To prepare cheesecakes using frozen blueberries, toss frozen berries with 2 Tbsp. all-purpose flour and 1 Tbsp. sugar.

Blueberry Cheesecake: Prepare recipe as directed through Step 2, pressing mixture onto bottom and 1½ inches up sides of a lightly greased 9-inch springform pan. Proceed with recipe as directed through Step 4, pouring batter into prepared pan. Proceed with recipe as directed, increasing bake time to 1 hour and 10 minutes or until almost set.

2	cups slivered almonds
1½	cups sugar, divided
3	Tbsp. butter, melted
4	Tbsp. all-purpose flour, divided
3	(8-oz.) packages cream cheese, softened
½	tsp. salt
4	large eggs
1	(8-oz.) container sour cream
1	tsp. vanilla extract
1	Tbsp. lemon zest
1½	cups fresh blueberries
1	cup whipping cream
2	tsp. sugar
2	Tbsp. sour cream

Garnishes: blueberries, lemon rind curls

Key Lime Cheesecake With Strawberry Sauce

makes 10 to 12 servings
prep: 20 min. • cook: 1 hr., 13 min. • other: 8 hr., 15 min.

2   cups graham cracker crumbs
¼   cup sugar
½   cup butter, melted
3   (8-oz.) packages cream cheese,
      softened
1¼   cups sugar
3   large eggs
1   (8-oz.) container sour cream
1½   tsp. lime zest
½   cup Key lime juice
Garnish: strawberries
Strawberry Sauce

1. Preheat oven to 350°. Stir together first 3 ingredients, and press on bottom and 1 inch up sides of a greased 9-inch springform pan. Bake at 350° for 8 minutes; let cool. Reduce oven temperature to 325°.

2. Beat cream cheese at medium speed with an electric mixer until fluffy; gradually add 1¼ cups sugar, beating until blended. Add eggs, 1 at a time, beating well after each addition. Stir in sour cream, zest, and juice. Pour batter into crust.

3. Bake at 325° for 1 hour and 5 minutes; turn oven off. Let stand in oven, with door partially open, 15 minutes. Remove from oven, and immediately run a knife around edge of pan, releasing sides.

4. Let cool completely in pan on a wire rack; cover and chill 8 hours. Garnish, if desired, and serve with Strawberry Sauce.

Strawberry Sauce:

makes 1 cup
prep: 5 min.

1¼   cups fresh strawberries
¼   cup sugar
1½   tsp. lime zest

1. Process all ingredients in a food processor until smooth, stopping to scrape down sides.

tip:
Fresh Key lime juice makes this authentic, but use bottled juice if fresh limes aren't available.

Eggnog Cheesecake with
Gingersnap Crust

Eggnog Cheesecake With Gingersnap Crust

holiday favorite

makes 12 servings
prep: 20 min. • **cook: 1 hr.** • **other: 9 hr., 30 min.**

1. Preheat oven to 325°. Stir together first 3 ingredients; press mixture onto bottom and up sides of a 10-inch springform pan.

2. Beat cream cheese at medium speed with an electric mixer until smooth; add eggs, 1 at a time, beating until blended after each addition. Add 1½ cups eggnog, and beat until blended. Fold in 2 cups powdered sugar and 2 Tbsp. flour; carefully pour cream cheese mixture into prepared pan.

3. Bake at 325° for 1 hour. Turn oven off. Let cheesecake stand in oven, with door closed, 1 hour. Remove to wire rack, and let cool completely. Cover and chill at least 8 hours.

4. Beat whipping cream at high speed with an electric mixer until stiff peaks form; fold in remaining ½ cup eggnog. Spread mixture evenly over top of chilled cheesecake, and garnish, if desired.

12 oz. gingersnaps (about 48 cookies), finely ground
¼ cup granulated sugar
¼ cup melted butter
32 oz. ⅓-less-fat cream cheese
4 large eggs
2 cups refrigerated or canned eggnog, divided
2 cups powdered sugar
2 Tbsp. all-purpose flour
1 cup whipping cream
Garnish: freshly grated nutmeg

Free-form Strawberry Cheesecake

photo on page 143

makes 6 servings
prep: 20 min.

1. Stir together strawberries and 2 Tbsp. powdered sugar.

2. Stir together cheesecake filling, lime zest, lime juice, and remaining 2 Tbsp. powdered sugar.

3. Spoon cheesecake mixture into 6 (6-oz.) glasses or ramekins. Sprinkle with crumbled cookies. Top with strawberry mixture. Garnish, if desired. Serve immediately.

Note: We tested with Philadelphia Ready-To-Eat Cheesecake Filling and Biscoff cookies.

2 cups fresh strawberries, sliced
4 Tbsp. powdered sugar, divided
1½ cups ready-to-eat cheesecake filling
1 tsp. lime zest
1 Tbsp. lime juice
6 crisp gourmet cookies, crumbled
Garnishes: crisp gourmet cookies, lime slices

Old-Fashioned Pies, Cobblers & Tarts

Get ready for some down-home comfort with our selection of freshly baked homemade sweets. From fruit to nuts to cream bases and everything in between, these choices will make it hard to decide which one to try first.

Apple, pumpkin, and pecan pie, oh my! While Southerners can't decide which filling is their favorite, we can agree on one thing—we love pie!

Pie—especially apple pie—is considered by many to be the iconic American dessert. Unfortunately, we can't take credit for it. In one form or another, pie has been around for over two thousand years. Ancient Egyptians were actually the first to make pastry-like crusts. The ancient Greeks eventually got hold of the idea, and the first pie recipe was published by the Romans. Over time, various pie recipes spread across Europe and made their way to America with the first English settlers. What you think of as pie today is likely very different from what was served in past times. In medieval England, "pyes" were typically filled with different meats, such as beef, lamb, duck—even pigeon. Fruit pies were introduced around the 1500s; fillings would consist of pears, apples, and quinces as opposed to the wild game of yesteryear.

More than any other single influence, Thomas Jefferson gave the upper South a touch of European culinary continentalism. Cream pie, napoleons, cherry tarts all came together at Monticello. It's to the cooks of the general population, however, not the plantation gentry that we owe the survival of delicious pies made from sweet potatoes, apples, and pecans—sweets that required little more than kitchen staples to assemble and that remain at the top of the list of regional favorites.

Among desserts, pies, cobblers, and tarts are Southern favorites. Cranberry-Apple Pie, Raspberry-Almond-Pear Tart, and Chocolate Icebox Pie are at the top of the list.

holiday favorite

2 ¼ lb. Granny Smith apples

2 ¼ lb. Braeburn apples

¼ cup all-purpose flour

2 Tbsp. apple jelly

1 Tbsp. fresh lemon juice

½ tsp. ground cinnamon

¼ tsp. salt

¼ tsp. ground nutmeg

⅓ cup sugar

Cornmeal Crust Dough

Wax paper

3 Tbsp. sugar

1 Tbsp. butter, cut into pieces

1 tsp. sugar

Brandy-Caramel Sauce

Double Apple Pie With Cornmeal Crust

Don't skip the apple jelly—it makes the baked pie juices taste rich. It also decreases the cloudiness that sometimes occurs with a flour-thickened apple pie filling.

makes 8 servings
prep: 30 min. • cook: 1 hr., 20 min. • other: 2 hr.

1. Preheat oven to 425°. Peel and core apples; cut into ½-inch-thick wedges. Place apples in a large bowl. Stir in next 7 ingredients. Let stand 30 minutes, gently stirring occasionally.

2. Place 1 Cornmeal Crust Dough disk on a lightly floured piece of wax paper; sprinkle dough lightly with flour. Top with another sheet of wax paper. Roll dough to about ⅛-inch thickness (about 11 inches wide).

3. Remove and discard top sheet of wax paper. Starting at 1 edge of dough, wrap dough around rolling pin, separating dough from bottom sheet of wax paper as you roll. Discard bottom sheet of wax paper. Place rolling pin over a 9-inch glass pie plate, and unroll dough over pie plate. Gently press dough into pie plate.

4. Stir apple mixture; reserve 1 Tbsp. juices. Spoon apples into crust, packing tightly and mounding in center. Pour remaining juices in bowl over apples. Sprinkle apples with 3 Tbsp. sugar; dot with butter.

5. Roll remaining Cornmeal Crust Dough disk as directed in Step 2, rolling dough to about ⅛-inch thickness (13 inches wide). Remove and discard wax paper, and place dough over filling; fold edges under, sealing to bottom crust, and crimp. Brush top of pie, excluding fluted edges, lightly with reserved 1 Tbsp. juices from apples; sprinkle with 1 tsp. sugar. Place pie on a jelly-roll pan. Cut 4 to 5 slits in top of pie for steam to escape.

6. Bake at 425° on lower oven rack 15 minutes. Reduce oven temperature to 350°; transfer pie to middle oven rack, and bake 35 minutes. Cover loosely with aluminum foil to prevent excessive browning, and bake 30 more minutes or until juices are thick and bubbly, crust is golden brown, and apples are tender when pierced with a long wooden pick through slits in crust. Remove to a wire rack. Cool 1½ to 2 hours before serving. Serve with Brandy-Caramel Sauce.

Cornmeal Crust Dough:

For a flaky crust, make sure the butter and shortening are cold. Our Food staff loved the flavor the apple cider brings to the crust.

makes 2 dough disks
prep: 15 min. • **other: 1 hr.**

1. Stir together first 4 ingredients in a large bowl. Cut butter and shortening into flour mixture with a pastry blender or fork until crumbly. Mound mixture on 1 side of bowl.

2. Drizzle 1 Tbsp. apple cider along edge of mixture in bowl. Using a fork, gently toss a small amount of flour mixture into cider just until dry ingredients are moistened; move mixture to other side of bowl. Repeat procedure with remaining cider and flour mixture.

3. Gently gather dough into 2 flat disks. Wrap in plastic wrap, and chill 1 to 24 hours.

2 ⅓ cups all-purpose flour
¼ cup plain yellow cornmeal
2 Tbsp. sugar
¾ tsp. salt
¾ cup cold butter, cut into ½-inch pieces
¼ cup chilled shortening, cut into ½-inch pieces
8 to 10 Tbsp. chilled apple cider

Brandy-Caramel Sauce:

We suggest using the full amount of butter in this sauce, although half of our tasting table thought it was fine with 2 Tbsp.

makes about 2 cups
prep: 5 min. • **cook: 5 min.** • **other: 10 min.**

1. Bring whipping cream to a light boil in a large saucepan over medium heat, stirring occasionally. Add sugar, and cook, stirring occasionally, 4 to 5 minutes or until sugar is dissolved and mixture is smooth. Remove from heat, and stir in butter, brandy, and vanilla. Let cool 10 minutes.

*Apple cider may be substituted.

1 cup whipping cream
1 ½ cups firmly packed brown sugar
2 Tbsp. to ¼ cup butter
2 Tbsp. brandy*
1 tsp. vanilla extract

Fresh Blackberry Pie

Though this pie should be assembled and served the same day, you can get a head start by combining the berries and sugar and chilling them the night before.

makes 8 servings
prep: 30 min. • **cook: 14 min.** • **other: 10 hr., 30 min.**

1. Gently toss berries and ¼ cup sugar in a large bowl; cover and chill 8 hours. Drain.

2. Preheat oven to 450°. Fit piecrust into a 9-inch pie plate according to package directions; fold edges under, and crimp. Prick bottom and sides of piecrust with a fork.

3. Bake at 450° for 7 to 9 minutes or until lightly browned.

4. Stir together cornstarch and remaining 1 cup sugar in a small saucepan; slowly whisk in 1¼ cups water and vanilla. Cook over medium heat, whisking constantly, 7 to 8 minutes or until mixture thickens.

5. Stir together raspberry gelatin and blue liquid food coloring in a small bowl; whisk into the warm cornstarch mixture.

6. Spoon blackberries into piecrust. Pour glaze evenly over berries, pressing down gently with a spoon to be sure all berries are coated. Chill 2½ hours. Serve with whipped cream, if desired.

1½ cups fresh blackberries
1¼ cups sugar, divided
½ (14.1-oz.) package refrigerated piecrusts
3 Tbsp. cornstarch
½ tsp. vanilla extract
1 (3-oz.) package raspberry gelatin
4 drops blue liquid food coloring
Sweetened whipped cream (optional)

Cranberry-Apple Pie

makes 8 servings
prep: 15 min. • **cook: 45 min.** • **other: 1 hr.**

1   (14.1-oz.) package refrigerated
    piecrusts, divided
1   large egg, lightly beaten
Cranberry-Apple Pie Filling
4   Tbsp. sparkling sugar, divided*

1. Preheat oven to 400°. Fit 1 piecrust into a 9-inch pie plate according to package directions. Brush edges of piecrust with egg. Spoon Cranberry-Apple Pie Filling into piecrust, mounding filling in center of pie.

2. Unroll remaining piecrust on a lightly floured surface. Brush piecrust lightly with egg; sprinkle with 2 Tbsp. sparkling sugar. Using the width of a ruler as a guide, cut the piecrust into 9 (1-inch-wide) strips. Arrange strips in a lattice design over filling; fold excess bottom piecrust under and along edges of top piecrust. Gently press ends of strips, sealing to bottom piecrust. Brush lattice with egg; sprinkle with remaining 2 Tbsp. sparkling sugar. Place pie on a baking sheet.

3. Bake at 400° on lower oven rack for 45 minutes, shielding with aluminum foil after 30 minutes to prevent excessive browning. Remove from oven, and let cool on a wire rack 1 hour.

*Regular or turbinado sugar may be substituted.

Cranberry-Apple Pie Filling:

makes enough for 1 (9-inch) pie
prep: 15 min. • **cook: 10 min.** • **other: 45 min.**

12   large apples, peeled (about 6 lb.)
1 ½   cups sugar
⅓   cup all-purpose flour
½   cup butter
1   cup sweetened dried cranberries

1. Cut apples into wedges; toss with 1½ cups sugar and ⅓ cup flour.

2. Melt butter in a large skillet over medium heat; add apple mixture to skillet, and sauté 10 to 15 minutes or until apples are tender. Stir in sweetened dried cranberries; remove from heat, and let cool 45 minutes or until completely cool.

tip:
Sparkling sugar can be found in specialty supermarkets and stores that carry cake-decorating supplies, or ordered online from www.wilton.com.

Fresh Georgia Peach Pie

makes 8 servings
prep: 30 min. • **cook: 40 min.** • **other: 1 hr.**

1. Preheat oven to 425°. Fit 1 piecrust into a 9-inch pie plate according to package directions.

2. Place peaches in a medium bowl; sprinkle with lemon juice, tossing gently. Combine granulated sugar and next 4 ingredients; sprinkle over peaches, tossing gently to coat.

3. Spoon filling into piecrust, and dot with butter. Top with remaining piecrust; fold edges under, and crimp. Cut several slits in top for steam to escape.

4. Bake at 425° for 15 minutes; shield edges with aluminum foil to prevent excessive browning. Bake 25 to 30 minutes or until golden brown. Let cool on a wire rack 1 hour.

*5 cups frozen peaches, thawed, may be substituted.

1	(14.1-oz.) package refrigerated piecrusts, divided
5	cups peeled, sliced fresh peaches*
1 ½	tsp. lemon juice
½	cup granulated sugar
½	cup firmly packed brown sugar
¼	cup all-purpose flour
½	tsp. ground cinnamon
¼	tsp. salt
2	Tbsp. butter, cut into small pieces

Blackberry Pudding Tarts

makes 16 tarts
prep: 25 min. • **cook: 15 min.** • **other: 1 hr.**

1. Bake tart shells according to package directions; cool 30 minutes or until completely cool.

2. Bring blackberries and 1 cup water to a boil in a large saucepan over medium heat. Reduce heat to medium-low, and simmer 5 minutes or until blackberries are soft.

3. Pour blackberry mixture through a wire-mesh strainer into a 4-cup liquid measuring cup, using back of a spoon to squeeze out juice to equal 2 cups. Discard pulp and seeds.

4. Combine 1½ cups sugar and ½ cup flour in a saucepan; gradually whisk in blackberry juice, whisking constantly until smooth. Bring to a boil over medium heat, whisking constantly. Reduce heat to low, and simmer 3 minutes or until thickened. Remove from heat.

5. Stir in butter and 2 tsp. vanilla. Spoon filling into prepared tart shells. Let cool 30 minutes or until completely cool.

6. Beat whipping cream at high speed with an electric mixer until foamy; gradually add remaining ¼ cup sugar, beating until stiff peaks form. Fold in remaining ⅛ tsp. vanilla. Dollop whipped cream over tarts; garnish, if desired.

*2 (12-oz.) packages frozen blackberries, thawed, may be substituted for fresh berries.

Note: We tested with VIP Pastry Shells.

2   (8-oz.) packages frozen tart
     shells
2   qt. fresh blackberries*
1 ¾ cups sugar, divided
½   cup self-rising flour
¼   cup butter, cut into pieces
2 ⅛ tsp. vanilla extract, divided
1   cup whipping cream
Garnishes: fresh blackberries, fresh
     mint sprigs

Fried Strawberry Pies

Freeze the pies before frying to prevent the crusts from disintegrating in the hot oil.

makes 36 pies
prep: 30 min. • **cook: 5 min. plus 2 min. per batch**
other: 1 hr., 20 min.

2　cups fresh strawberries, hulled and mashed
¾　cup granulated sugar
¼　cup cornstarch
2　(14.1-oz.) packages refrigerated piecrusts
Vegetable oil
Powdered sugar
Garnish: sliced strawberries

1. Bring first 3 ingredients to a boil in a saucepan over medium heat. Cook, stirring constantly, 1 minute or until thickened. Let cool completely (about 20 minutes).

2. Unroll 1 piecrust on a lightly floured surface. Roll into a 13- x 12-inch rectangle. Cut into 9 circles with a 3½-inch round cutter. Moisten edges with water. Spoon 2 teaspoons strawberry mixture into the center of each circle; fold piecrust over filling, pressing edges with a fork to seal. Repeat procedure with remaining piecrusts and strawberry mixture.

3. Place pies in a single layer on baking sheets. Freeze 1 to 8 hours.

4. Pour oil to a depth of 1 inch into a large heavy skillet; heat to 350°. Fry pies, in batches, 1 minute on each side or until golden. Drain on paper towels; sprinkle with powdered sugar. Garnish, if desired.

Spoon the strawberry mixture into the center of each dough circle. Use your fingers to fold dough over.

Gently press edges to seal with the tines of a fork.

Make sure your oil has reached 350° before frying the pies. If it's not hot enough, the pies will be too oily. Use a slotted spoon to remove golden-fried pies, and drain on paper towels.

Double Citrus Tart

makes 8 to 10 servings
prep: 30 min. • **cook: 20 min.** • **other: 4 hr.**

1. Preheat oven to 325°. Stir together first 4 ingredients. Press mixture evenly into a 9-inch tart pan with removable bottom; set aside.

2. Whisk together sweetened condensed milk, orange juice concentrate, lemon juice, and egg yolks until blended.

3. Beat egg whites at medium speed with an electric mixer until stiff peaks form; fold into condensed milk mixture. Pour into prepared crust.

4. Bake at 325° for 20 to 25 minutes or just until filling is set. Let cool completely on a wire rack. Cover and chill at least 4 hours. Remove tart from pan, and place on a serving dish.

5. Beat whipping cream and granulated sugar at medium speed with an electric mixer until stiff peaks form. Dollop around edges of tart; garnish, if desired.

1 ½ cups crushed gingersnap cookies
5 Tbsp. butter, melted
2 Tbsp. brown sugar
¼ tsp. ground cinnamon
1 (14-oz.) can sweetened condensed milk
⅓ cup frozen orange juice concentrate, thawed
¼ cup fresh lemon juice
2 large eggs, separated
1 cup heavy whipping cream
3 Tbsp. granulated sugar
Garnishes: lemon and orange zest strips

Grapefruit Tart

Ruby Red grapefruit is sweeter than larger varieties. Choose those that are firm, thin-skinned, and heavy for their size—they provide the most juice and best flavor. One medium grapefruit yields about ⅔ cup juice.

makes 8 servings
prep: 30 min. • cook: 20 min. • other: 2 hr., 30 min.

1	(5.3-oz.) package pure butter shortbread
3	Tbsp. sugar
2	Tbsp. butter, melted
½	cup sugar
6	Tbsp. cornstarch
⅛	tsp. salt
2	cups fresh red grapefruit juice
4	egg yolks
3	Tbsp. butter
2	tsp. red grapefruit zest
3	red grapefruit, peeled and sectioned
2	Tbsp. sugar

1. Preheat oven to 350°. Process shortbread in a blender or food processor 30 seconds or until graham cracker crumb consistency (about 1⅓ cup crumbs). Stir together shortbread crumbs, 3 Tbsp. sugar, and 2 Tbsp. melted butter in a small bowl. Press mixture lightly onto bottom and up sides of a greased 9-inch tart pan.

2. Bake at 350° for 10 to 12 minutes or until lightly browned.

3. Combine ½ cup sugar, 6 Tbsp. cornstarch, and ⅛ tsp. salt in a medium-size heavy saucepan. Whisk in fresh grapefruit juice and egg yolks. Cook over medium-high heat, whisking constantly, 10 to 12 minutes or until mixture thickens and boils. Remove from heat; stir in 3 Tbsp. butter and 2 tsp. red grapefruit zest.

4. Pour filling into prepared tart shell. Place plastic wrap directly on filling (to prevent a film from forming). Chill 2½ hours.

5. Place red grapefruit sections in an 8-inch baking dish. Sprinkle with 2 Tbsp. sugar; cover and chill until ready to assemble tart. Drain grapefruit sections.

6. Arrange grapefruit sections over tart, slightly overlapping to cover filling completely. Serve immediately. Cover and chill any remaining tart up to 3 days.

Note: We tested with Walkers Pure Butter Shortbread and TexaSweet Ruby Red Texas grapefruit.

tip:
To make this tart ahead, prepare the crust and filling up to 2 days ahead, but do not top with fruit. Top with grapefruit just before serving.

To section grapefruit, use a sharp, thin-bladed knife to cut a ¼-inch-thick slice from each end of grapefruit.

Place grapefruit, one flat end down, on a cutting board; remove peel in strips. Remove any bitter white pith.

Hold peeled grapefruit in palm of your hand; slice between membranes. Gently remove whole segments.

Rustic Plum Tart

If the plums are very ripe, their juices may ooze out of the tart and onto the parchment paper, but this adds to the dessert's charm.

makes 8 servings
prep: 20 min. • **cook: 50 min.** • **other: 50 min.**

1. Preheat oven to 350°. Line a baking sheet with parchment paper; coat parchment paper with cooking spray.

2. Stir together plums and next 4 ingredients in a large bowl. Let stand 30 minutes, stirring occasionally.

3. Unroll piecrust on prepared baking sheet. Roll into a 12-inch circle.

4. Drain plum mixture, reserving liquid. Toss plums in flour.

5. Mound plums in center of piecrust, leaving a 3-inch border. Fold piecrust border up and over plums, pleating as you go, leaving an opening about 5 inches wide in center.

6. Stir together egg and 1 Tbsp. water. Brush piecrust with egg mixture, and sprinkle with 1 Tbsp. sugar.

7. Bake at 350° for 45 minutes or until filling is bubbly and crust is golden. Carefully transfer tart on parchment paper to a wire rack; cool 20 minutes.

8. Meanwhile, bring reserved plum liquid to a boil in a small saucepan over medium heat. Boil 1 to 2 minutes or until slightly thickened. Let cool slightly. Brush or drizzle 1 to 2 Tbsp. hot plum liquid over exposed fruit in center of tart. Serve immediately with remaining plum syrup, and, if desired, Sweet Cream Topping.

Sweet Cream Topping:

1. Stir together sour cream and brown sugar. Cover and chill 2 hours before serving. Stir just before serving.

Parchment paper
Vegetable cooking spray
1 ½ lb. plums, sliced
½ cup sugar
⅓ cup plum preserves
1 tsp. vanilla extract
¼ tsp. ground allspice
½ (14.1-oz.) package refrigerated piecrusts
1 Tbsp. all-purpose flour
1 large egg
1 Tbsp. sugar
Sweet Cream Topping (optional)

½ cup sour cream
2 tsp. brown sugar

Raspberry-Almond-Pear Tart

makes 6 to 8 servings
prep: 20 min. • **cook: 44 min.** • **other: 50 min.**

⅓ cup plus 1 Tbsp. slivered almonds

½ (14.1-oz.) package refrigerated piecrusts

⅓ cup seedless raspberry jam

6 Tbsp. butter, softened and divided

4 large pears, peeled and cut into eighths

¼ cup sugar

1 large egg

⅓ cup finely crushed vanilla wafers (about 12)

¼ tsp. almond extract

1. Preheat oven to 350°. Bake almonds in a single layer in a shallow pan 4 to 5 minutes or until toasted and fragrant. Let cool 10 minutes. Increase oven temperature to 400°. Pulse almonds in a food processor 15 seconds or until finely ground.

2. Fit piecrust into a 9-inch tart pan; trim excess. Freeze piecrust 10 minutes.

3. Bake at 400° for 10 minutes; remove from oven to a wire rack, and cool 30 minutes or until completely cool. Spread raspberry jam on bottom of prepared crust.

4. Melt 2 Tbsp. butter in a large skillet over medium-high heat; add pears, and cook, stirring often, 5 minutes. Remove from heat, and arrange pears in a spoke pattern over raspberry jam.

5. Beat remaining 4 Tbsp. butter at medium speed with an electric mixer until creamy; gradually add sugar, beating well. Add egg, beating until blended. Stir in crushed vanilla wafers, ground almonds, and almond extract; spread over pears.

6. Bake at 400° for 25 minutes or until browned. Cool on a wire rack.

Strawberry Tart

This summertime dessert is made even better with the addition of vanilla bean paste.

makes 6 to 8 servings
prep: 20 min. • **cook: 32 min.** • **other: 2 hr.**

4	oz. cream cheese, softened
½	cup butter, softened
1	Tbsp. sugar
¼	tsp. salt
1¼	cups all-purpose flour
Parchment paper	
½	cup sugar
¼	cup cornstarch
2	cups half-and-half
4	egg yolks
3	Tbsp. butter
½	tsp. vanilla bean paste*
1	qt. fresh strawberries, sliced

1. Preheat oven to 400°. Beat first 4 ingredients at medium speed with an electric mixer until creamy. Add flour, and beat at low speed until a dough forms. Shape into a disk; cover and chill 30 minutes.

2. Place dough on a lightly floured surface; sprinkle lightly with flour. Roll dough between 2 sheets of plastic wrap to ⅛-inch thickness. Starting at 1 edge of dough, wrap dough around a rolling pin, separating dough from bottom sheet of plastic wrap as you roll. Discard bottom sheet of plastic wrap. Place rolling pin over a 9-inch tart pan, and unroll dough over pan. Remove top sheet of plastic wrap. Press dough onto bottom and up sides of a 9-inch tart pan. Gently roll or press rolling pin against edges of tart pan to remove excess dough. Line dough with parchment paper, and fill with pie weights or dried beans.

3. Bake at 400° for 17 minutes. Remove weights and parchment paper, and bake 5 more minutes or until lightly browned.

4. Combine ½ cup sugar and ¼ cup cornstarch in a heavy saucepan. Whisk together half-and-half and egg yolks. Gradually whisk half-and-half mixture into sugar mixture in saucepan over medium heat. Bring to a boil, and cook, whisking constantly, 1 minute. Remove from heat.

5. Stir in 3 Tbsp. butter and ½ tsp. vanilla bean paste. Place plastic wrap directly on filling in saucepan (to prevent a film from forming). Let stand 30 minutes or until set.

6. Spoon into prepared shell. Cover and chill 1 hour or until completely cool. Top with fresh strawberry slices. Store in refrigerator.

*½ tsp. vanilla extract may be substituted.

Roll dough between two sheets of plastic wrap to ⅛-inch thickness.

Wrap dough around rolling pin, separating dough from bottom sheet of plastic wrap.

Gently roll or press rolling pin against edges of tart pan to remove excess dough.

Press vanilla wafer crumb mixture firmly on bottom, up sides, and onto lip of pie plate.

Arrange half of banana slices over bottom of crust.

Spread final layer of hot Vanilla Cream Filling over layers of bananas, filling, and vanilla wafers; proceed as directed.

Banana Pudding Pie

kids love it

makes 8 servings
prep: 20 min. • cook: 20 min. • other: 5 hr., 30 min.

1. Preheat oven to 350°. Set aside 30 vanilla wafers; pulse remaining vanilla wafers in a food processor 8 to 10 times or until coarsely crushed. (Yield should be about 2½ cups.) Stir together crushed vanilla wafers and butter until blended. Firmly press on bottom, up sides, and onto lip of a 9-inch pie plate.

2. Bake at 350° for 10 to 12 minutes or until lightly browned. Remove to a wire rack, and cool completely (about 30 minutes).

3. Arrange half of banana slices evenly over bottom of crust. Prepare Vanilla Cream Filling, and spread half of hot filling over bananas; top with 20 vanilla wafers. Spread ¾ cup hot filling over vanilla wafers, and top with remaining half of banana slices. Spread remaining hot filling (about 1 cup) over banana slices. (Filling will be about ¼ inch higher than top edge of crust.)

4. Beat egg whites at high speed with an electric mixer until foamy. Add sugar, 1 Tbsp. at a time, beating until stiff peaks form and sugar dissolves. Spread meringue evenly over hot filling, sealing the edges.

5. Bake at 350° for 10 to 12 minutes or until golden brown. Remove from oven, and let cool on wire rack until completely cool (about 1 hour). Coarsely crush remaining 10 vanilla wafers, and sprinkle evenly over top of pie. Chill at least 4 hours. Store in refrigerator.

Note: We tested with Nabisco Nilla Wafers.

1	(12-oz.) box vanilla wafers, divided
½	cup butter, melted
2	large bananas, sliced
	Vanilla Cream Filling
4	egg whites
½	cup sugar

Vanilla Cream Filling:

makes about 3 cups
prep: 5 min. • cook: 8 min.

1. Whisk together first 5 ingredients in a heavy saucepan. Cook over medium-low heat, whisking constantly, 8 to 10 minutes or until mixture reaches the thickness of chilled pudding. (Mixture will just begin to bubble and will be thick enough to hold soft peaks when whisk is lifted.) Remove from heat, and stir in vanilla. Use filling immediately.

¾	cup sugar
⅓	cup all-purpose flour
2	large eggs
4	egg yolks
2	cups milk
2	tsp. vanilla extract

Coconut Cream Pie

makes 8 servings
prep: 20 min. • **cook: 27 min.** • **other: 1 hr., 15 min.**

1. Preheat oven to 425°. Fit 1 piecrust into a 9-inch pie plate according to package directions; fold edges under, and crimp. Prick bottom and sides of piecrust with a fork. Bake at 425° for 12 to 15 minutes or until lightly browned. Let cool on a wire rack.

2. Combine ½ cup sugar and cornstarch in a heavy saucepan. Whisk together half-and-half and egg yolks. Gradually whisk egg mixture into sugar mixture; bring to a boil over medium heat, whisking constantly. Boil 1 minute; remove from heat. Stir in butter, 1 cup coconut, and 1 tsp. vanilla. Place plastic wrap directly on warm custard (to prevent a film from forming); let stand 30 minutes.

3. Remove and discard plastic wrap. Spoon custard mixture into crust; cover and chill 30 minutes or until set.

4. Preheat oven to 350°. Place 3 Tbsp. coconut in a single layer in a shallow pan; bake 5 to 6 minutes or until toasted, stirring occasionally. Cool completely (about 15 minutes).

5. Beat whipping cream at high speed with an electric mixer until foamy; gradually add ⅓ cup sugar and remaining 1½ tsp. vanilla, beating until soft peaks form. Spread or pipe whipped cream over pie filling. Sprinkle with toasted coconut. Store in refrigerator.

holiday favorite

½	(14.1-oz.) package refrigerated piecrusts
½	cup sugar
¼	cup cornstarch
2	cups half-and-half
4	egg yolks
3	Tbsp. butter
1	cup sweetened flaked coconut
2 ½	tsp. vanilla extract, divided
3	Tbsp. sweetened flaked coconut
2	cups whipping cream
⅓	cup sugar

Lemon Chess Pie

makes 8 servings
prep: 10 min. • **cook: 57 min.** • **other: 1 hr., 30 min.**

1. Preheat oven to 425°. Fit piecrust into a 9-inch pie plate according to package directions; fold edges under, and crimp. Line with aluminum foil, and fill with pie weights or dried beans.

2. Bake at 425° for 5 minutes. Remove weights and foil. Bake 2 more minutes or until light golden brown. Cool on a wire rack 30 minutes or until completely cool. Reduce oven temperature to 350°.

3. Prepare Lemon Chess Pie Filling, and pour into prepared crust.

4. Bake at 350° for 50 minutes or until pie is firm, shielding edges with aluminum foil to prevent excess browning, if needed. Cool on a wire rack 1 hour or until completely cool. Garnish, if desired. Store in refrigerator.

Lemon Chess Pie Filling:

makes about 3 cups
prep: 10 min.

1. Whisk together all ingredients. Use filling immediately.

½ (15-oz.) package refrigerated
    piecrusts
Lemon Chess Pie Filling
Garnishes: whipped cream, lemon
    rind curls

2 cups sugar
4 large eggs
¼ cup butter, melted
¼ cup milk
1 Tbsp. lemon zest
¼ cup fresh lemon juice
1 Tbsp. all-purpose flour
1 Tbsp. white cornmeal
¼ tsp. salt

Historically, peanuts have been an abundant cash crop in Virginia, Georgia, and Alabama. By the late 1800s in the South, locally made peanut butter was sold door to door in Northeastern states. It wasn't until the 1920s that peanut butter was produced commercially.

Peanut Butter Pie

makes 8 servings
prep: 15 min. • **cook: 23 min.** • **other: 3 hr.**

1 ¼ cups graham cracker crumbs
⅓ cup dry-roasted peanuts, coarsely ground
2 Tbsp. granulated sugar
¼ cup plus 2 Tbsp. butter, melted
⅔ cup granulated sugar
3 Tbsp. cornstarch
¼ tsp. salt
2 ½ cups evaporated milk
2 egg yolks, lightly beaten
½ cup peanut butter
½ cup peanut butter morsels
1 tsp. vanilla extract
½ cup whipping cream
1 Tbsp. powdered sugar
¼ tsp. vanilla extract
Chopped dry-roasted peanuts

1. Preheat oven to 350°. Combine first 3 ingredients; stir in melted butter. Firmly press crumb mixture into a lightly greased 9-inch pie plate.

2. Bake at 350° for 8 minutes or until browned. Set aside to cool.

3. Combine ⅔ cup granulated sugar, cornstarch, and salt in a heavy saucepan. Gradually stir in evaporated milk. Cook over medium heat, stirring constantly, until mixture is thickened and bubbly. Gradually stir about one-fourth of hot mixture into beaten egg yolks; add to remaining hot mixture, stirring constantly. Cook, stirring constantly with a wire whisk, 3 minutes or until thickened. Remove from heat. Stir in peanut butter, morsels, and 1 tsp. vanilla. Stir until morsels melt.

4. Pour filling into prebaked crust. Cover and chill pie 3 hours or until firm. Store in refrigerator.

5. Beat whipping cream at medium speed with an electric mixer until foamy; add powdered sugar and ¼ tsp. vanilla, and beat until soft peaks form. Top each serving with whipped cream, and sprinkle with chopped peanuts.

Eggnog Pie

This dessert is like a "black bottom" eggnog pie.

makes 8 servings
prep: 17 min. • **cook: 22 min.** • **other: 4 hr., 6 min.**

2   cups pecan shortbread cookie
    crumbs (about 18 cookies)
¼   cup butter, melted
½   cup semisweet chocolate
    morsels
2 ¼ cups whipping cream
⅓   cup granulated sugar
½   cup bourbon or rum
½   tsp. freshly grated nutmeg
1   envelope unflavored gelatin
¼   cup cold water
6   egg yolks, lightly beaten
1   Tbsp. butter
Freshly grated nutmeg
Powdered sugar
Unsweetened whipped cream
    (optional)

1. Preheat oven to 350°. Stir together cookie crumbs and ¼ cup melted butter; press firmly into a greased 9-inch deep-dish pie plate. Bake at 350° for 8 minutes. Remove crust from oven, and sprinkle chocolate morsels into warm crust. Let stand 5 minutes or until morsels melt; carefully spread chocolate over bottom of crust with a spatula. Set aside.

2. Stir together whipping cream and next 3 ingredients in top of a double boiler; bring water just to a simmer. Cook over simmering water 6 to 8 minutes or until thoroughly heated.

3. Meanwhile, sprinkle gelatin over cold water in a small bowl; let stand 1 minute.

4. Gradually whisk one-fourth of warm cream mixture into egg yolks. Add to remaining warm cream, whisking constantly. Whisk in softened gelatin. Cook over simmering water 3 to 5 minutes or until custard reaches 160°. Remove from heat; add 1 Tbsp. butter, stirring gently until butter melts. Cool filling to room temperature.

5. Pour filling into prepared crust. Gently cover with plastic wrap, pressing directly on surface of filling. Chill pie at least 4 hours or until firm.

6. Sprinkle nutmeg and powdered sugar over pie before serving. Serve with dollops of whipped cream and more nutmeg, if desired. Store pie in refrigerator.

Note: We tested with Keebler Pecan Sandies.

tip:
The chocolate layer will harden as the pie chills in the refrigerator. Use a sharp knife and gentle pressure to slice the pie.

Sweet Potato Pie

makes 16 servings

prep: 10 min. • cook: 1 hr., 41 min. • other: 15 min.

2   lb. sweet potatoes
1   (14.1-oz.) package refrigerated
     piecrusts
½   cup butter, softened
3   large eggs
⅔   cup firmly packed light brown
     sugar
⅓   cup granulated sugar
½   cup sweetened condensed milk
½   cup evaporated milk
1   Tbsp. fresh lemon juice
1   tsp. vanilla extract
½   tsp. ground cinnamon
⅛   tsp. ground nutmeg

1. Preheat oven to 400°. Bake sweet potatoes 50 to 55 minutes or until tender; remove from oven, and let cool 15 minutes. Increase oven temperature to 425°.

2. Meanwhile, fit 1 piecrust into each of 2 (9-inch) pie plates according to package directions. Line with aluminum foil, and fill each with pie weights or dried beans.

3. Bake at 425° for 7 minutes. Remove weights and foil, and bake 4 more minutes. Remove piecrusts to a wire rack. Decrease oven temperature to 350°.

4. Cut sweet potatoes in half lengthwise. Scoop out pulp into bowl of an electric mixer. Beat sweet potatoes and butter at medium speed until smooth. Add eggs and next 8 ingredients, beating well. Pour mixture evenly into prepared piecrusts.

5. Bake at 350° on lower oven rack 40 to 45 minutes or until set, shielding edges with aluminum foil to prevent excessive browning, if necessary. Store in refrigerator.

Pineapple Meringue Pie

Pineapple, like lemon juice, is acidic and will prevent the cornstarch from thickening properly if added before the custard is cooked. Chilling the pie after it cools to room temperature further sets the filling and makes for perfect slices.

makes 8 servings
prep: 20 min. • **cook: 28 min.** • **other: 6 hr.**

1. Preheat oven to 350°. Stir together cookie crumbs, 1 cup coconut, and ¼ cup melted butter; firmly press on bottom, up sides, and onto lip of a lightly greased 9-inch pie plate.

2. Bake at 350° for 10 to 12 minutes or until lightly browned. Remove to a wire rack, and let cool 1 hour or until completely cool.

3. Whisk together milk and cornstarch in a heavy saucepan, whisking until cornstarch is dissolved. Whisk in egg yolks and ¾ cup sugar, whisking until blended. Cook over medium-low heat, whisking constantly, 8 to 10 minutes or until a chilled pudding-like thickness. (Mixture will just begin to bubble and will be thick enough to hold soft peaks when whisk is lifted.) Remove from heat; stir in pineapple, 1 Tbsp. butter, and vanilla. Spoon immediately into cooled piecrust.

4. Beat egg whites at high speed with an electric mixer until foamy. Add remaining ¼ cup sugar, 1 Tbsp. at a time, beating until stiff peaks form and sugar is dissolved. Spread meringue over hot filling, sealing edges. Sprinkle remaining ⅓ cup of coconut over meringue.

5. Bake at 350° for 10 to 12 minutes or until golden brown. Remove from oven to wire rack, and let cool 1 hour or until completely cool. Chill at least 4 hours. Store in refrigerator.

2	cups pecan shortbread cookie crumbs
1⅓	cups sweetened flaked coconut, divided
¼	cup butter, melted
2	cups milk
¼	cup cornstarch
3	large eggs, separated
1	cup sugar, divided
1	(20-oz.) can crushed pineapple, drained
1	Tbsp. butter
1	tsp. vanilla extract

Lemon Meringue Pie

makes 8 to 10 servings
prep: 25 min. • **cook: 32 min.** • **other: 1 hr.**

½ (14.1-oz.) package refrigerated
    piecrusts
Lemon Meringue Pie Filling
6   egg whites
½   tsp. vanilla extract
6   Tbsp. sugar

1. Preheat oven to 425°. Fit piecrust into a 9-inch pie plate according to package directions; fold edges under, and crimp. Prick bottom and sides of piecrust with a fork.

2. Bake at 425° for 12 to 15 minutes or until crust is lightly browned, shielding edges with aluminum foil to prevent excessive browning, if necessary. Remove crust to a wire rack. Reduce oven temperature to 325°.

3. Prepare Lemon Meringue Pie Filling; pour into prepared crust. Cover with plastic wrap, placing directly on filling (to prevent a film from forming). (Proceed immediately to next step to ensure that meringue is spread over pie while filling is hot.)

4. Beat egg whites and vanilla at high speed with an electric mixer until foamy. Add sugar, 1 Tbsp. at a time, and beat 2 to 4 minutes or until stiff peaks form and sugar is dissolved.

5. Remove plastic wrap from pie, and spread meringue over warm filling, sealing edges.

6. Bake at 325° for 20 to 25 minutes or until golden brown. Cool on wire rack 1 hour or until completely cool. Store in refrigerator.

Pour cooked Lemon Meringue Pie Filling into prepared piecrust.

Beat egg whites and vanilla until foamy; add sugar, 1 Tbsp. at a time, beating until stiff peaks form.

Spread meringue over warm Lemon Meringue Pie Filling, sealing edges.

Lemon Meringue Pie Filling:

makes enough for 1 (9-inch) pie
prep: 10 min. • **cook: 10 min.**

1. Whisk together first 3 ingredients in a heavy, nonaluminum, medium saucepan. Whisk together egg yolks, milk, and lemon juice in a bowl; whisk into sugar mixture in pan over medium heat. Bring to a boil, and boil, whisking constantly, 1 minute. Remove pan from heat; stir in butter, lemon zest, and vanilla until smooth. Use filling immediately.

1	cup sugar
¼	cup cornstarch
⅛	tsp. salt
4	egg yolks
2	cups milk
⅓	cup fresh lemon juice
3	Tbsp. butter
1	tsp. lemon zest
½	tsp. vanilla extract

Butterscotch Tarts

kids love it

makes 12 servings
prep: 30 min. • **cook: 30 min.** • **other: 2 hr., 20 min.**

1. Prepare tart shells according to package directions.

2. Combine cornstarch and 2 Tbsp. cold water in a small saucepan, stirring until smooth. Stir in ½ cup hot water; cook over medium heat, stirring constantly, until mixture thickens and boils (about 3 to 4 minutes). Boil, stirring constantly, 1 minute. Remove from heat; let cool completely (about 20 minutes).

3. Preheat oven to 325°. Combine brown sugar and next 3 ingredients in a large heavy saucepan. Whisk together egg yolks, milk, butter, and ⅔ cup water; gradually whisk into brown sugar mixture until smooth.

4. Cook over medium heat, whisking constantly, until mixture thickens and boils (about 10 minutes). Boil, whisking constantly, 1 minute. Remove from heat; stir in 1 tsp. vanilla. Pour into tart shells.

5. Beat egg whites at medium speed with an electric mixer until foamy. Combine 3 Tbsp. granulated sugar and ¼ tsp. baking powder; gradually add mixture to egg whites, 1 Tbsp. at a time, beating until stiff peaks form and sugar is dissolved. Add cornstarch mixture and remaining 1 tsp. vanilla; beat until blended. Spread meringue over warm filling in tart shells, sealing to edges of shells.

6. Bake at 325° for 15 to 20 minutes or until golden brown. Let cool completely (about 2 hours). Store in refrigerator.

1 ½ (8-oz.) packages frozen tart shells
1   Tbsp. cornstarch
2   Tbsp. cold water
½   cup hot water
1   cup firmly packed light brown sugar
½   cup granulated sugar
⅓   cup all-purpose flour
Pinch of salt
3   large eggs, separated
1 ⅓ cups milk
2   Tbsp. butter, melted
2   tsp. vanilla extract, divided
3   Tbsp. granulated sugar
¼   tsp. baking powder

old-fashioned pies, cobblers & tarts

Key Lime Pie

Southerners debate whether key lime pies should have a pastry crust or a graham cracker crust and whether the topping should be meringue or sweetened whipped cream. But folks typically agree that the best version is the one before them.

makes 8 servings
prep: 30 min. • **cook: 32 min.** • **other: 8 hr., 30 min.**

1 ¼ cups graham cracker crumbs
⅓ cup butter, melted
¼ cup firmly packed light brown sugar
2 (14-oz.) cans sweetened condensed milk
1 cup fresh Key lime juice
2 egg whites
¼ tsp. cream of tartar
2 Tbsp. granulated sugar

1. Preheat oven to 350°. Combine first 3 ingredients. Press on bottom and up sides of a 9-inch pie plate. Bake at 350° for 10 minutes. Let cool 30 minutes or until completely cool. Reduce oven temperature to 325°.

2. Stir together sweetened condensed milk and Key lime juice until blended. Pour into prepared crust.

3. Beat egg whites and cream of tartar at high speed with an electric mixer just until foamy. Add sugar, 1 Tbsp. at a time, beating until soft peaks form and sugar is dissolved (2 to 4 minutes). Spread meringue over filling, sealing edges.

4. Bake at 325° for 22 to 25 minutes. Cover and chill at least 8 hours. Store in refrigerator.

Scrubby, thorned Key lime trees grow in almost every backyard in the subtropical Florida Keys, but after a 1926 hurricane wiped out the citrus groves, growers found less temperamental and thornless Persian lime trees easier to grow. Still, the juice from the newer varieties can't replace that of the small, tart, seedy Key limes necessary for the traditional pie that is pale yellow, never green.

Chocolate-Key Lime Cupcake Pies

makes 1 dozen
prep: 30 min. • **cook: 20 min.** • **other: 4 hr., 30 min.**

12 jumbo-size aluminum foil baking cups

Vegetable cooking spray

1 (9-oz.) package chocolate wafer cookies

½ cup butter, melted

3 (8-oz.) packages cream cheese, softened

1½ cups sugar

2 tsp. Key lime zest

⅓ cup fresh Key lime juice

3 large eggs

Garnishes: sweetened whipped cream, fresh cherries and blackberries, fresh mint leaves

1. Preheat oven to 350°. Place 12 jumbo-size aluminum foil baking cups in lightly greased muffin pans, and coat with cooking spray.

2. Pulse chocolate wafer cookies in a food processor 8 to 10 times or until finely crushed. Stir together cookie crumbs and butter; firmly press on bottom and two-thirds up sides of each baking cup (about 3 Tbsp. crumbs per cup).

3. Beat cream cheese and sugar at medium speed with an electric mixer until blended. Add lime zest and lime juice, beating at low speed until well blended. Add eggs, 1 at a time, beating just until yellow disappears after each addition. Spoon mixture into prepared cups, filling completely full.

4. Bake at 350° for 20 minutes or until set. Cool in pans on wire racks 15 minutes. Remove from pans to wire racks, and cool completely (about 15 minutes). Cover and chill at least 4 hours. Store in refrigerator. Garnish, if desired.

Peach Melba Ice-Cream Pie

makes 6 to 8 servings
prep: 10 min. • **cook: 5 min.** • **other: 8 hr.**

2   Tbsp. slivered almonds
1   (1.75-qt.) container peach ice
     cream
1   (8-oz.) container sour cream
3   Tbsp. grenadine
Vanilla Wafer Crust
Raspberry Sauce

1. Preheat oven to 350°. Bake almonds in a single layer in a shallow pan 5 to 6 minutes or until toasted and fragrant.

2. Remove packaging from ice cream using scissors. Cut ice cream into 8 pieces; place in bowl of a heavy-duty electric stand mixer. (Do not use a handheld mixer.)

3. Stir together sour cream and grenadine. Add to ice cream in bowl. Beat at low speed until softened and combined. Spoon into chilled Vanilla Wafer Crust. Sprinkle with almonds. Freeze 8 hours, covering pie once ice cream is frozen. Serve with Raspberry Sauce.

Note: We tested with Breyers Peach Ice Cream. Grenadine may be found on the drink mix aisle of the grocery store. We do not recommend using a handheld mixer in this recipe; beating the firm ice cream will burn up the motor.

Vanilla Wafer Crust:

makes 1 (9-inch) piecrust
prep: 15 min. • **cook: 17 min.** • **other: 1 hr.**

½   cup slivered almonds
2   cups vanilla wafer crumbs
½   cup butter, melted

1. Preheat oven to 350°. Bake almonds in a single layer in a shallow pan 7 to 8 minutes or until toasted and fragrant. Let cool 15 minutes or until completely cool. Process almonds in a food processor 30 seconds or until finely chopped.

2. Stir together vanilla wafer crumbs, butter, and almonds. Press firmly on bottom and up sides of a 9- or 9½-inch deep-dish pie plate.

3. Bake at 350° for 10 to 12 minutes or until golden brown. Cool crust on a wire rack 30 minutes or until completely cool. Freeze 15 minutes before filling.

Raspberry Sauce:

makes 1 cup
prep: 5 min. • **cook: 10 min.** • **other: 1 hr.**

1. Combine first 3 ingredients and, if desired, orange liqueur in a small saucepan. Bring to a boil over medium-high heat; reduce heat to medium, and simmer, uncovered, 5 minutes or just until raspberry mixture starts to thicken.

2. Stir together cornstarch and 1 Tbsp. water in a small bowl. Whisk into raspberry mixture, and cook 1 minute. Remove from heat; pour mixture through a fine wire-mesh strainer into a bowl. Discard solids. Cover and chill 1 hour before serving.

*1 (12-oz.) package frozen raspberries, thawed, may be substituted. Proceed with recipe as directed. Sauce will be a little thinner and less sweet. Makes 1¼ cups.

Note: We tested with Cointreau for orange liqueur.

1	(10-oz.) package frozen raspberries, thawed*
½	cup sugar
3	Tbsp. lemon juice
1	Tbsp. orange liqueur (optional)
1	tsp. cornstarch

Strawberry Smoothie Ice-Cream Pie

makes 10 to 12 servings
prep: 50 min. • **cook: 10 min.** • **other: 5 hr., 5 min.**

1   (7-oz.) package waffle cones, broken into pieces
6   Tbsp. butter, melted
1   Tbsp. granulated sugar
2   (1-qt.) containers premium vanilla ice cream
1   (16-oz.) container fresh strawberries, stemmed
¼   cup powdered sugar, divided
1   pt. fresh blueberries
2   ripe bananas
Garnishes: fresh halved strawberries, fresh blueberries, fresh mint sprigs

1. Preheat oven to 350°. Process first 3 ingredients in a food processor 10 seconds or until finely crushed. Firmly press mixture onto bottom of a lightly greased 10-inch springform pan.

2. Bake at 350° for 10 minutes. Cool completely in pan on a wire rack 30 minutes or until completely cool.

3. Meanwhile, let vanilla ice cream stand at room temperature 20 minutes or until slightly softened.

4. Process strawberries and 2 Tbsp. powdered sugar in a food processor 10 seconds or until pureed, stopping to scrape down sides. Transfer strawberry mixture to a bowl.

5. Process blueberries and 1 Tbsp. powdered sugar in food processor 10 seconds or until pureed, stopping to scrape down sides. Transfer blueberry mixture to a bowl.

6. Process bananas and remaining 1 Tbsp. powdered sugar in food processor 10 seconds or until pureed, stopping to scrape down sides. Transfer banana mixture to a bowl.

7. Place 1 qt. vanilla ice cream in a large bowl; cut into 3-inch pieces. Fold strawberry mixture into ice cream until blended. Place ice-cream mixture in freezer until slightly firm.

8. Divide remaining 1 qt. ice cream equally between 2 separate bowls. Stir blueberry mixture into ice cream in 1 bowl and banana mixture into ice cream in remaining bowl. Place bowls in freezer. Stir occasionally.

9. Spread half of strawberry mixture into prepared crust in springform pan. Place pan and remaining strawberry mixture in bowl in freezer. Freeze 30 minutes or until strawberry layer in pan is slightly firm.

10. Spread banana mixture over strawberry layer in pan; return pan to freezer, and freeze 30 minutes or until banana layer is slightly firm. Repeat procedure with blueberry mixture.

11. Meanwhile, let remaining strawberry mixture stand at room temperature 15 minutes, stirring occasionally. Spread remaining strawberry mixture over blueberry layer in pan, and freeze 3 hours or until all layers are firm. (Cover pie once ice cream is frozen.) Let pie stand at room temperature 15 minutes before serving. Garnish, if desired.

Note: We tested with Häagen-Dazs ice cream.

tip: Stirring the banana and blueberry mixtures occasionally while freezing the strawberry layer in Step 9 will ensure that they stay soft enough to spread. Be sure to let the strawberry mixture stand at room temperature before spreading on top of the pie (as directed in Step 11); otherwise it will be too firm to spread.

Place strawberry mixture, blueberry mixture, and banana mixture in separate bowls.

Cut ice cream into 3-inch pieces; fold in strawberry mixture until blended.

Spread blueberry mixture over frozen banana layer in pan, and freeze 30 minutes.

Grasshopper Pie

makes 8 servings
prep: 18 min. • **other: 9 hr., 30 min.**

1. Process cookies in a food processor or blender until ground; add butter, and process until blended. Reserve ½ cup crumb mixture. Firmly press remaining crumb mixture in an ungreased 13- x 9-inch pan. Chill 30 minutes.

2. Spoon ice cream over crust; cover and freeze 1 hour. Stir together whipped topping, powdered sugar, and vanilla; spread over ice cream layer. Sprinkle remaining ½ cup crumb mixture over whipped topping mixture. Cover and freeze at least 8 hours.

30	cream-filled chocolate sandwich cookies
⅓	cup butter, melted
½	gal. mint chocolate chip ice cream, softened
1	(8-oz.) container frozen whipped topping, thawed
½	cup sifted powdered sugar
½	tsp. vanilla extract

tip:
Soften the ice cream at room temperature for about 10 to 15 minutes so it will spread easily over the crust. If time is tight, soften it in the microwave at MEDIUM LOW (30% power) for about 20 to 30 seconds.

3   (2.07-oz.) chocolate-coated
    caramel-peanut nougat bars
1   baked Pretzel Crust
1½ (8-oz.) packages cream cheese,
    softened
½   cup sugar
⅓   cup sour cream
⅓   cup creamy peanut butter
2   large eggs
⅔   cup semisweet chocolate
    morsels
2   Tbsp. whipping cream
¼   cup coarsely chopped, lightly
    salted peanuts

2   cups finely crushed pretzel sticks
¼   cup firmly packed light brown
    sugar
¾   cup melted butter

Candy Bar Pie

makes 8 servings
prep: 20 min. • cook: 35 min. • other: 3 hr.

1. Preheat oven to 325°. Cut candy bars into ¼-inch pieces; arrange over bottom of crust.

2. Beat cream cheese and sugar at medium speed with an electric mixer until blended. Add sour cream and peanut butter, beating at low speed until well blended. Add eggs, 1 at a time, beating just until yellow disappears after each addition. Spoon cream cheese mixture over candy on crust.

3. Bake at 325° for 35 to 40 minutes or until set. Remove to a wire rack, and let cool 1 hour or until completely cool. Cover and chill 2 hours.

4. Microwave chocolate and cream in a microwave-safe bowl at HIGH for 30 seconds or until melted and smooth, stirring at 15-second intervals. Drizzle over top of cooled pie, and sprinkle evenly with peanuts.

Note: We tested with Snickers candy bars.

Pretzel Crust:

makes 1 (9-inch) crust
prep: 10 min. • cook: 10 min. • other: 1 hr.

1. Preheat oven to 350°. Stir together all ingredients; firmly press crumb mixture on bottom, up sides, and onto lip of a lightly greased 9-inch pie plate. Bake at 350° for 10 to 12 minutes or until lightly browned. Remove to a wire rack, and cool crust 1 hour or until completely cool before filling.

Chocolate Icebox Pie

chocolate decadence

A quick sprinkling of coarsely chopped candy bars and toasted pecans sends this pie to the table in style.

makes 8 servings
prep: 20 min. • **cook: 13 min.** • **other: 8 hr., 35 min.**

1. Cook milk in a heavy, nonaluminum 3-qt. saucepan over medium heat, stirring often, 6 to 8 minutes or just until bubbles appear. (Do not boil.) Remove from heat, and whisk in chocolate morsels until melted. Cool slightly (about 5 minutes).

2. Stir together ¼ cup cold water and 2 Tbsp. cornstarch until dissolved. Whisk cornstarch mixture, sweetened condensed milk, eggs, and vanilla into chocolate mixture. Bring to a boil over medium heat, whisking constantly. Boil 1 minute or until mixture thickens and is smooth. (Do not overcook.)

3. Remove from heat, and whisk in butter. Pour mixture into piecrust. (Pie will be very full.) Cover and chill at least 8 hours.

4. Preheat oven to 350°. Bake pecans in a single layer in a shallow pan 5 minutes or until toasted and fragrant. Cool completely in pan on a wire rack (about 30 minutes).

5. Beat whipping cream at high speed with an electric mixer until foamy; gradually add sugar, beating until soft peaks form. Mound whipped cream in center of pie, and sprinkle with chopped candy bar. Sprinkle toasted pecans around edge of pie. Store in refrigerator.

⅔ cup milk
¾ cup semisweet chocolate morsels
¼ cup cold water
2 Tbsp. cornstarch
1 (14-oz.) can sweetened condensed milk
3 large eggs, beaten
1 tsp. vanilla extract
3 Tbsp. butter
1 (6-oz.) ready-made chocolate crumb piecrust
½ cup chopped pecans
1 cup whipping cream
¼ cup sugar
1 (1.55-oz.) milk chocolate candy bar, chopped

Chocolate-Peanut Butter Ice-Cream Pie

makes 6 to 8 servings
prep: 20 min. • **cook: 13 min.** • **other: 7 hr.**

21   cream-filled chocolate sandwich
     cookies
½   cup unsalted dry-roasted peanuts
¼   cup butter, melted
3   pt. chocolate ice cream, softened
8   (1.5-oz.) packages peanut butter
     cup candies, coarsely chopped
¾   cup fudge sauce
¼   cup strong brewed coffee
2   Tbsp. coffee liqueur (optional)
Garnish: chopped unsalted dry-
     roasted peanuts

1. Preheat oven to 350°. Process cookies and ½ cup peanuts in a food processor 30 seconds or until finely crumbled. Add melted butter, and process 15 seconds or until blended. Press crumb mixture into a 9-inch deep-dish pie plate. Bake at 350° for 10 minutes. Let cool on a wire rack 30 minutes. Freeze 15 minutes.

2. Stir together chocolate ice cream and chopped candies; spoon into piecrust. Freeze 6 hours, covering pie once ice cream is frozen.

3. Heat fudge sauce in a small saucepan over low heat, stirring constantly, 3 to 4 minutes or until thoroughly heated. Remove from heat; stir in coffee and, if desired, coffee liqueur. Let pie stand at room temperature 15 minutes before serving. Serve sauce with pie. Garnish, if desired.

Note: We tested with Oreo Sandwich Cookies, Blue Bell Chocolate Ice Cream, and Reese's Peanut Butter Cup candies.

Fudgy Peanut Butter Cup Pie

Pies that require chilling or freezing make excellent desserts for entertaining because you can prepare them in advance and then forget about them until serving time. For an impressive presentation, carefully transfer this frozen pie from the aluminum pie plate to a serving plate.

makes 8 servings
prep: 15 min. • **other: 2 hr., 30 min.**

1. Allow container of ice cream to stand at room temperature 20 to 30 minutes to soften.

2. Spread peanut butter over crust; freeze 10 minutes.

3. Spread softened ice cream evenly over peanut butter in crust. Arrange peanut butter cup candy halves, cut sides down, around edges of crust. Drizzle chocolate-peanut butter shell coating over ice cream. Freeze at least 2 hours.

4. Cut frozen pie with a warm knife to serve.

Note: We tested with Mayfield Moose Tracks Ice Cream.

tip:

The secret to frozen pies is not to freeze pies as hard as a rock, but to freeze them long enough so they're firm enough for slicing and soft enough to spoon into.

1   (1.75-qt.) container vanilla ice cream with peanut butter cups swirled with fudge

⅓   cup creamy or chunky peanut butter

1   (6-oz.) ready-made chocolate crumb piecrust

6   (0.55-oz.) peanut butter cup candies, halved

½   cup chocolate-peanut butter shell coating

Tiramisù Toffee Trifle Pie

makes 8 to 10 servings
prep: 25 min. • **other: 8 hr.**

1½ Tbsp. instant coffee granules
¾ cup warm water
1 (10.75-oz.) frozen pound cake, thawed
1 (8.8-oz.) package cream cheese or mascarpone, softened
½ cup powdered sugar
½ cup chocolate syrup
1 (12-oz.) container frozen whipped topping, thawed and divided
2 (1.4-oz.) English toffee candy bars, coarsely chopped*

1. Stir together coffee granules and ¾ cup warm water until coffee granules are dissolved. Let cool.

2. Meanwhile, cut cake into 14 slices. Cut each slice in half crosswise. Place cake slices in bottom and overlapping up sides of a 9-inch deep-dish pie plate. Drizzle coffee mixture over cake slices.

3. Beat cream cheese, sugar, and chocolate syrup at medium speed with an electric mixer until smooth. Add 2½ cups whipped topping, and beat until light and fluffy.

4. Spread cheese mixture evenly over cake. Top pie with remaining whipped topping. Sprinkle with chopped candy bars. Cover and chill 8 hours.

*10 miniature English toffee candy bars (from 1 [12-oz.] package), coarsely chopped, may be substituted.

Note: Tiramisù Toffee Trifle Pie may be made the day before serving. Store in the refrigerator.

Fudge Truffle-Pecan Tart

This tart is also delicious served with a dollop of sweetened whipped cream.

makes 10 to 12 servings
prep: 20 min. • **cook: 20 min.** • **other: 1 hr.**

1. Preheat oven to 375°. Microwave chocolate in a microwave-safe bowl at HIGH 1½ minutes or until chocolate is melted and smooth, stirring at 30-second intervals.

2. Beat brown sugar and butter at medium speed with an electric mixer until blended; add eggs, beating well. Stir in melted chocolate, vanilla, and next 3 ingredients. Pour batter into prepared Chocolate Tart Shell.

3. Bake at 375° for 20 minutes. Let cool on a wire rack 1 hour. Garnish, if desired.

Chocolate Tart Shell:

makes 1 (11-inch) crust
prep: 5 min. • **cook: 6 min.** • **other: 30 min.**

1. Preheat oven to 350°.

2. Combine chocolate graham cracker crumbs and melted butter; press onto bottom of an 11-inch tart pan with removable bottom.

3. Bake at 350° for 6 minutes. Let cool on a wire rack 30 minutes or until completely cool.

*Chocolate-flavored teddy bear-shaped graham crackers, crushed, may be substituted.

Note: We tested with Nabisco Chocolate Teddy Graham Snacks.

1	(12-oz.) package semisweet chocolate morsels
¾	cup firmly packed light brown sugar
½	cup butter, softened
3	large eggs
1	tsp. vanilla extract
1	cup finely chopped pecans
½	cup all-purpose flour
2	tsp. instant coffee granules
	Chocolate Tart Shell
	Garnish: shaved chocolate curls

1¼	cups chocolate graham cracker crumbs*
⅓	cup melted butter

Elegant Pumpkin-Walnut Layered Pie

A pecan pie-like layer nestles beneath the creamy pumpkin topping.

makes 8 servings
prep: 20 min. • **cook: 1 hr.** • **other: 1 hr.**

1 cup chopped walnuts
1 (14.1-oz.) package refrigerated piecrusts, divided
1 large egg, lightly beaten
3 Tbsp. butter, melted
¼ tsp. vanilla extract
1¼ cups firmly packed light brown sugar, divided
1 (8-oz.) package cream cheese, softened
2 large eggs
1 (15-oz.) can pumpkin
2 Tbsp. all-purpose flour
1 tsp. ground cinnamon
½ tsp. ground ginger
½ tsp. ground allspice
¼ tsp. ground nutmeg
Vanilla ice cream (optional)

1. Preheat oven to 350°. Bake walnuts in a single layer in a shallow pan 8 to 10 minutes or until toasted and fragrant, stirring occasionally. Remove from oven; increase oven temperature to 425°.

2. Unroll 1 piecrust, and cut out pastry leaves using a 2-inch leaf-shaped cutter. Brush leaves with beaten egg. Place leaves on an ungreased baking sheet.

3. Bake at 425° for 6 to 7 minutes or until golden. Let cool on a wire rack.

4. Meanwhile, fit remaining piecrust into a 9-inch pie plate according to package directions; fold edges under, and crimp. Prick bottom and sides of piecrust with a fork.

5. Bake at 425° for 6 to 8 minutes or until lightly browned.

6. Combine toasted walnuts, butter, vanilla, and ½ cup brown sugar; spread walnut mixture in bottom of prepared piecrust.

7. Beat cream cheese at medium speed with an electric mixer until creamy. Gradually add remaining ¾ cup brown sugar, beating well. Add eggs and pumpkin, beating well.

8. Combine flour and next 4 ingredients; add to cream cheese mixture, beating until blended. Pour cream cheese filling over walnut layer.

9. Bake at 425° for 10 minutes. Reduce oven temperature to 350°, and bake 30 to 35 more minutes or until pie is set. Let cool on wire rack 1 hour. Arrange pastry leaves around edge of pie. Serve chilled with vanilla ice cream, if desired.

Caramel-Pecan Pie

makes 8 servings
prep: 20 min. • **cook: 49 min.** • **other: 1 hr.**

1. Preheat oven to 350°. Bake pecans in a single layer in a shallow pan 8 to 10 minutes or until lightly toasted and fragrant, stirring occasionally. Remove from oven; increase oven temperature to 425°.

2. Fit 1 piecrust into a 9-inch pie plate according to package directions; fold edges under, and crimp. Prick bottom and sides of piecrust with a fork.

3. Unroll remaining piecrust on a lightly floured surface. Cut piecrust into 6 (12- x ¼-inch) strips. Twist 2 strips loosely around each other. Repeat with remaining strips. Brush edge of piecrust lightly with beaten egg. Arrange twisted piecrust strips on edge of crust, pressing gently to adhere.

4. Bake at 425° for 6 to 8 minutes or until very lightly browned; let cool on a wire rack. Reduce oven temperature to 400°.

5. Combine caramels, butter, and ¼ cup water in a large saucepan over medium heat. Cook, stirring constantly, 5 to 7 minutes or until caramels and butter are melted; remove from heat.

6. Stir together sugar and next 3 ingredients. Stir into caramel mixture until thoroughly combined. Stir in toasted pecans. Pour into prepared crust.

7. Bake at 400° for 10 minutes. Reduce heat to 350°, and bake 20 more minutes, shielding edges of crust with aluminum foil to prevent excessive browning. Let cool on wire rack 1 hour.

1   cup coarsely chopped pecans
1   (14.1-oz.) package refrigerated
      piecrusts, divided
1   large egg, lightly beaten
28   caramels
¼   cup butter
¾   cup sugar
2   large eggs
½   tsp. vanilla extract
¼   tsp. salt

Of the many kinds of nut pies that appear on Southern tables, pecan is probably the most often served. It wasn't until after the Civil War, when pecan trees began to flourish across the Southern states, that this favorite pie was born. Today, Georgia is the country's top producer of pecans, which come from the only major nut tree native to the U.S.

Mom's Pecan Pie

makes 8 servings
prep: 10 min. • **cook: 1 hr., 3 min.**

1½   cups pecan halves*
1   (14.1-oz.) package refrigerated
     piecrusts, divided
3   large eggs
1   cup sugar
¾   cup light or dark corn syrup
2   Tbsp. melted butter
2   tsp. vanilla extract
½   tsp. salt

1. Preheat oven to 350°. Bake pecans in a single layer in a shallow pan 8 to 10 minutes or until toasted.

2. Unroll and stack 2 piecrusts; gently roll or press together. Fit into a 9-inch pie plate according to package directions; fold edges under and crimp.

3. Stir together eggs and next 5 ingredients; stir in pecans. Pour filling into pie shell.

4. Bake at 350° for 55 minutes or until set, shielding pie with aluminum foil after 20 minutes to prevent excessive browning. Serve warm or cold.

*Chopped pecans may be substituted for pecan halves.

Note: We tested with Mrs. Smith's Deep Dish Frozen Pie Shell.

Fudge Pie

No crust needed for this dense brownie sensation. Just slice it into wedges and crown it with ice cream, chocolate syrup, and pecans.

makes 8 servings
prep: 12 min. • **cook: 35 min.**

1. Preheat oven to 350°. Cook butter and chocolate in a small saucepan over low heat, stirring often until melted.

2. Beat eggs at medium speed with an electric mixer 5 minutes. Gradually add sugar, beating until blended. Gradually add chocolate mixture, flour, and vanilla, beating until blended. Stir in ½ cup pecans.

3. Pour mixture into a lightly greased 9-inch pie plate.

4. Bake at 350° for 35 to 40 minutes or until center is firm. Let cool. Top each serving with vanilla ice cream and chocolate syrup; sprinkle with remaining chopped pecans.

¾ cup butter
3 (1-oz.) unsweetened chocolate squares
3 large eggs
1½ cups sugar
¾ cup all-purpose flour
1 tsp. vanilla extract
¾ cup chopped pecans, toasted and divided
Toppings: vanilla ice cream, chocolate syrup

Apple-Gingerbread Cobbler

makes 8 servings
prep: 15 min. • **cook: 35 min.**

1 (14.5-oz.) package gingerbread
   mix, divided
¼ cup firmly packed light brown
   sugar
½ cup butter, divided
½ cup chopped pecans
2 (21-oz.) cans apple pie filling
Vanilla ice cream (optional)

1. Preheat oven to 375°. Stir together 2 cups gingerbread mix and ¾ cup water until smooth.

2. Stir together remaining gingerbread mix and brown sugar; cut in ¼ cup butter with a pastry blender or fork until mixture is crumbly. Stir in pecans.

3. Combine apple pie filling and remaining ¼ cup butter in a large saucepan, and cook over medium heat, stirring often, 5 minutes or until thoroughly heated.

4. Spoon hot apple mixture into a lightly greased 11- x 7-inch baking dish. Spoon gingerbread-water mixture over hot apple mixture; sprinkle with gingerbread-pecan mixture.

5. Bake at 375° for 30 to 35 minutes or until set. Serve cobbler with vanilla ice cream, if desired.

Blackberry Cobbler

kids love it

makes 6 to 8 servings
prep: 10 min. • **cook: 45 min.**

1. Preheat oven to 425°. Stir together first 4 ingredients in a large bowl. Gently stir in blackberries until sugar mixture is crumbly. Spoon fruit mixture into a lightly greased 11- x 7-inch baking dish.

2. Cut piecrust into ½-inch-wide strips, and arrange strips diagonally over blackberry mixture. Sprinkle with 1 Tbsp. sugar.

3. Bake at 425° for 45 minutes or until crust is golden brown and center is bubbly.

¾ cup sugar
½ cup all-purpose flour
½ cup butter, melted
2 tsp. vanilla extract
2 (12-oz.) bags frozen blackberries, unthawed (about 5 cups)
½ (14.1-oz.) package refrigerated piecrusts
1 Tbsp. sugar

Caramel-Applesauce Cobbler With Bourbon-Pecan Ice Cream

This recipe was inspired by an applesauce pie with hard sauce that Test Kitchens staffer Mary Allen Perry enjoyed at her grandmother's house as a child. After devouring it, family members may drift away from the table to doze off.

makes 8 servings
prep: 45 min. • **cook: 40 min.**

½ cup butter
12 large Granny Smith apples, peeled and sliced
2 cups sugar
2 Tbsp. lemon juice
1 (14.1-oz.) package refrigerated piecrusts
Bourbon-Pecan Ice Cream

1. Preheat oven to 425°. Melt butter in a large Dutch oven over medium-high heat. Add apples, sugar, and lemon juice; cook, stirring often, 20 to 25 minutes or until apple is caramel-colored. Spoon into a shallow, greased 2-qt. baking dish.

2. Cut each piecrust into ½-inch strips. Arrange strips in a lattice design over filling; fold edges under. Place remaining strips on a baking sheet.

3. Bake remaining strips at 425° for 8 to 10 minutes or until golden. Bake cobbler at 425° for 20 to 25 minutes or until crust is golden. Serve warm with pastry strips and Bourbon-Pecan Ice Cream.

Bourbon-Pecan Ice Cream:

makes 2 pt.
prep: 5 min. • **other: 4 hr.**

2 pt. homemade-style vanilla ice cream, softened
1 cup chopped toasted pecans
¼ cup bourbon

1. Stir together all ingredients; freeze at least 4 hours.

Note: We tested with Blue Bell Homemade Vanilla Ice Cream.

Too-Easy Cherry Cobbler

Save even more time by using store-bought, crustless white bread for the topping.

makes 4 to 6 servings
prep: 15 min. • **cook: 35 min.**

1. Preheat oven to 350°. Stir together pie filling, cherries, and 2 Tbsp. flour. Stir in almond extract. Place in a lightly greased 8-inch square baking dish.

2. Trim crusts from bread slices; cut each slice into 5 strips. Arrange bread strips over fruit mixture in baking dish.

3. Stir together sugar, next 3 ingredients, and remaining 2 Tbsp. flour; drizzle mixture over bread strips.

4. Bake at 350° for 35 to 45 minutes or until golden and bubbly.

Too-Easy Peach Cobbler: Substitute 2 (16-oz.) packages frozen peaches, thawed and drained, for cherry pie filling and canned cherries. Omit almond extract and lemon zest. Proceed with recipe as directed.

Too-Easy Berry Cobbler: Substitute 1 (21-oz.) can blueberry pie filling and 2 (10-oz.) packages frozen whole strawberries, unthawed, for cherry pie filling and canned cherries. Substitute 1 tsp. vanilla extract and 1 tsp. lemon juice for almond extract. Proceed with recipe as directed.

2	(21-oz.) cans cherry pie filling
1	(15-oz.) can pitted dark sweet cherries in heavy syrup, drained
¼	cup all-purpose flour, divided
½	tsp. almond extract
5	white bread slices
1 ¼	cups sugar
½	cup butter, melted
1	large egg
1 ½	tsp. lemon zest

Though cobblers made with meat were popular in England, colonial Southerners learned to make cobbler for dessert using what was available—peaches, apples, and berries. The best place to cool a juicy cobbler was on a wide windowsill, where the tantalizing aroma enticed kids to come in for supper on time.

Double-Crust Peach Cobbler

makes 8 servings
prep: 30 min. • **cook: 37 min.** • **other: 20 min.**

8   cups sliced fresh peaches (about 5 lb.)*
2   cups sugar
3   Tbsp. all-purpose flour
½   tsp. ground nutmeg
1   tsp. almond or vanilla extract
⅓   cup butter
Double-Crust Pastry, divided
2   tsp. milk
2   tsp. sugar

1. Preheat oven to 475°. Stir together first 4 ingredients in a Dutch oven; let stand until syrup forms (about 20 minutes). Bring peach mixture to a boil over medium-high heat; reduce heat to low, and cook, stirring occasionally, 10 minutes or until tender. Remove from heat; stir in almond extract and butter, stirring until butter is melted.

2. Roll 1 Double-Crust Pastry portion to ⅛-inch thickness on a lightly floured surface; cut into a 9-inch square. Spoon half of peach mixture into a lightly buttered 2-qt. baking dish; top with pastry square.

3. Bake at 475° for 12 to 14 minutes or until lightly browned. Spoon remaining peach mixture over baked pastry square.

4. Roll remaining Double-Crust Pastry portion to ⅛-inch thickness on a lightly floured surface, and cut into 1-inch strips; arrange in lattice design over peaches. Brush with 2 tsp. milk, and sprinkle with 2 tsp. sugar. Bake 15 to 18 more minutes or until golden brown.

* 2 (20-oz.) packages frozen unsweetened peach slices, thawed, may be substituted.

Double-Crust Pastry:

makes 1 double-crust pastry
prep: 8 min.

1. Combine flour and salt; cut in shortening with a pastry blender or fork until mixture is crumbly. Sprinkle with ice water, 1 Tbsp. at a time, stirring with a fork until dry ingredients are moistened. Shape into a ball. Wrap in plastic wrap, and chill until ready to use.

2	cups all-purpose flour
1	tsp. salt
⅔	cup shortening
4	to 6 Tbsp. ice water

Sweet Potato Cobbler

Enjoy sweet potatoes in this rustic biscuit-topped cobbler. For an added Southern tradition, drizzle some heavy cream over each serving, or top with a scoop of vanilla ice cream.

makes 8 servings
prep: 25 min. • **cook: 50 min.**

1. Preheat oven to 350°. Melt ½ cup butter in a 10½-inch cast-iron skillet over medium heat. Whisk in whipping cream and next 5 ingredients. Remove from heat.

2. Add sweet potatoes, and spread evenly in skillet. Cover with aluminum foil, and place on a baking sheet. Bake at 350° for 25 to 30 minutes or until sweet potatoes are tender. Uncover.

3. Cut ⅓ cup butter into flour with a pastry blender until crumbly; add buttermilk, stirring just until dry ingredients are moistened. Turn dough out onto a lightly floured surface; gently knead 3 to 4 times. Pat or roll dough into a 10½-inch circle; place over cobbler. Sprinkle with Pecan Streusel Topping.

4. Bake, uncovered, at 350° for 25 minutes or until golden. Garnish, if desired.

½	cup butter
2	Tbsp. whipping cream
1	cup granulated sugar
¼	cup firmly packed light brown sugar
1	tsp. ground cinnamon
¼	tsp. ground nutmeg
¼	tsp. salt
2	large sweet potatoes, peeled and thinly sliced (about 2 lb.)
⅓	cup butter
1 ⅔	cups self-rising flour
½	cup buttermilk
	Pecan Streusel Topping
	Garnish: whipped topping

Pecan Streusel Topping:

makes 1⅔ cups
prep: 5 min.

1. Combine first 3 ingredients; cut in butter with a pastry blender or fork until crumbly. Stir in chopped pecans.

⅓	cup uncooked regular oats
⅓	cup all-purpose flour
⅓	cup firmly packed light brown sugar
¼	cup cold butter, cut into pieces
⅓	cup chopped pecans

8   white bread slices, cut into
     ¼-inch cubes
⅓   cup butter, melted
1   cup firmly packed brown sugar
1   Tbsp. ground cinnamon
4   large Granny Smith apples,
     peeled and cut into ¼-inch-thick
     slices
1   cup apple cider

½   (14.1-oz.) package refrigerated
     piecrusts
1   (12-oz.) package frozen spiced
     apples, thawed
1   egg white, lightly beaten
Sugar
1   (12-oz.) jar butterscotch topping,
     warmed

Apple Brown Betty

makes 6 servings
prep: 15 min. • **cook: 55 min.** • **other: 10 min.**

1. Preheat oven to 350°. Pulse bread cubes in a food processor 8 to 10 times or until mixture resembles fine crumbs.

2. Stir together breadcrumbs and butter in small bowl.

3. Stir together brown sugar and cinnamon. Place half of apple slices in a lightly greased 8-inch square baking dish; sprinkle apples evenly with half of brown sugar mixture and half of breadcrumb mixture. Repeat procedure with remaining apples, brown sugar mixture, and breadcrumb mixture. Pour apple cider evenly over top.

4. Bake at 350° for 55 minutes. Let stand 10 minutes before serving.

Quick Apple Bundles

makes 4 servings
prep: 10 min. • **cook: 18 min.**

1. Preheat oven to 425°. Unfold piecrust according to package directions. Cut into fourths. Place apples evenly in center of each fourth. Pull corners over apples, pinching to seal. Place on a baking sheet; brush evenly with egg white, and sprinkle with sugar.

2. Bake at 425° for 18 to 20 minutes or until golden. Serve warm with butterscotch topping.

Note: We tested with Stouffer's Harvest Apples.

Apple Brown Betty

Sweet Breads & Coffee Cakes

Don't miss out on these wonderfully scrumptious sweet breads! Try Bananas Foster Upside-Down Coffee Cake for a tasty twist on the classic Southern dessert. If you're in the mood for warm, crunchy goodness, enjoy a slice of Caramel-Nut Pull-Apart Bread. No matter what the occasion, these recipes are perfect for entertaining any crowd.

If Southerners know how to enjoy one thing, it's sweets. From breakfast to dessert, we satisfy our sugar cravings with the most delicious of sweet breads—scones, coffee cakes, and bread puddings, just to name a few.

While bread dates back to the earliest days of civilization, sweet breads are a rather recent development in culinary history. The Scottish scone, traditionally a breakfast or tea bread, has been around since the 1500s. Scones were originally flat yeast cakes. Made with unleavened oats, the cakes were scored into wedges and cooked on a griddle. Modern versions are similar to rich biscuits and are usually made with flour and baked in an oven. Coffee cake, which is more a bread than it is a cake, probably originated in Europe during the 17th century when coffee was introduced. Sweet breads served as the perfect accompaniment to this new drink, and by

1879, countless coffee cake recipes showed up in cookbooks across America. Southerners still enjoy their morning cup o' joe with a delicious slice of coffee cake. Another Southern favorite, bread pudding was once called "poor man's pudding" as it was made from stale leftover bread. Today, we know bread pudding as a rich, decadent dessert that has graced the menus of many fine establishments throughout the South. From sun up to sun down, there's never a bad time to enjoy sweets in the South.

Lemon Tea Bread, Bananas Foster Upside-Down Coffee Cake, and Blueberry 'n' Cheese Coffee Cake will make any morning brighter.

Praline-Apple Bread

Sour cream is the secret to the rich, moist texture of this bread. There's no butter or oil in the batter—only in the glaze.

makes 1 loaf
prep: 20 min. • **cook: 1 hr., 10 min.** • **other: 1 hr., 10 min.**

1. Preheat oven to 350°. Bake ½ cup pecans in a single layer in a shallow pan 6 to 8 minutes or until toasted and fragrant, stirring after 4 minutes.

2. Beat sour cream and next 3 ingredients at low speed with an electric mixer 2 minutes or until blended.

3. Stir together flour and next 3 ingredients. Add to sour cream mixture, beating just until blended. Stir in apples and ½ cup toasted pecans. Spoon batter into a greased and floured 9- x 5-inch loaf pan. Sprinkle with remaining 1 cup chopped pecans; lightly press pecans into batter.

4. Bake at 350° for 1 hour to 1 hour and 5 minutes or until a wooden pick inserted in center comes out clean, shielding with aluminum foil after 50 minutes to prevent excessive browning. Cool in pan on a wire rack 10 minutes; remove from pan to wire rack.

5. Bring butter and brown sugar to a boil in a 1-qt. heavy sauce-pan over medium heat, stirring constantly; boil 1 minute. Remove from heat, and spoon over top of bread; let cool completely (about 1 hour).

Note: To freeze Praline-Apple Bread, cool it completely; wrap in plastic wrap, then in aluminum foil. Freeze up to 3 months. Thaw at room temperature.

1½ cups chopped pecans, divided
1 (8-oz.) container sour cream
1 cup granulated sugar
2 large eggs
1 Tbsp. vanilla extract
2 cups all-purpose flour
2 tsp. baking powder
½ tsp. baking soda
½ tsp. salt
1½ cups peeled, finely chopped Granny Smith apples (about ¾ lb.)
½ cup butter
½ cup firmly packed light brown sugar

Cream Cheese-Banana-Nut Bread

To get perfect slices, let the bread cool 30 minutes and then cut with a serrated or electric knife.

1 ¼   cups chopped pecans, divided
¼   cup butter, softened
1   (8-oz.) package ⅓-less-fat cream
      cheese, softened
1   cup sugar
2   large eggs
1 ½   cups whole wheat flour*
1 ½   cups all-purpose flour
½   tsp. baking powder
½   tsp. baking soda
½   tsp. salt
1   cup buttermilk
1 ½   cups mashed very ripe bananas
      (1 ¼ lb. unpeeled bananas,
      about 4 medium)
½   tsp. vanilla extract

makes 2 loaves
prep: 15 min. • **cook: 1 hr., 12 min.** • **other: 40 min.**

1. Preheat oven to 350°. Bake ¾ cup pecans in a single layer in a shallow pan 12 to 15 minutes or until toasted and fragrant, stirring after 6 minutes.

2. Beat butter and cream cheese at medium speed with an electric mixer until creamy. Gradually add sugar, beating until light and fluffy. Add eggs, 1 at a time, beating just until blended after each addition.

3. Combine whole wheat flour and next 4 ingredients; gradually add to butter mixture alternately with buttermilk, beginning and ending with flour mixture. Beat at low speed just until blended after each addition. Stir in bananas, ¾ cup toasted pecans, and vanilla. Spoon batter into 2 greased and floured 8- x 4-inch loaf pans. Sprinkle with remaining ½ cup pecans.

4. Bake at 350° for 1 hour or until a long wooden pick inserted in center comes out clean and sides of bread pull away from pan, shielding with aluminum foil during last 15 minutes to prevent excessive browning, if necessary. Let cool in pans on wire racks 10 minutes. Remove from pans to wire racks, and cool 30 minutes.

Note: To make ahead, proceed with recipe as directed through Step 4. Cool loaves completely, and tightly wrap with plastic wrap. Wrap again with aluminum foil. Freeze up to 1 month.

*When working with whole wheat flour, be aware that accurate measuring is essential. Be sure to spoon the flour into a dry measuring cup (do not pack) rather than scooping the cup into the flour, and level it off with a straight edge. Expect a denser bread with this recipe. It won't rise as much as traditional breads, and the texture will be very moist.

tip:

To bake muffins, spoon batter evenly into 24 paper-lined muffin cups. Bake at 350° for 25 minutes or until a wooden pick inserted in center comes out clean. Cool in pans 10 minutes. Remove from pans, and cool completely on wire racks. Makes 24 muffins. Prep: 15 min., Bake: 25 min.

Orange-Pecan-Topped Cream Cheese-Banana-Nut Bread:
Prepare bread batter as directed, and spoon into desired pans.
Sprinkle 1 cup coarsely chopped, toasted pecans evenly over
batter in pans. Bake as directed. Cool bread or muffins in pans
10 minutes; remove from pans to wire racks. Stir together 1 cup
powdered sugar, 3 tablespoons fresh orange juice, and 1 teaspoon
grated orange rind until blended. Drizzle evenly over warm bread
or muffins, and cool 30 minutes on wire racks.

**Peanut Butter Streusel-Topped Cream Cheese-Banana-Nut
Bread:** Prepare bread batter as directed, and spoon into desired
pans. Combine ½ cup plus 1 tablespoon all-purpose flour and
½ cup firmly packed brown sugar in a small bowl. Cut in ¼ cup
butter and 3 tablespoons creamy peanut butter with a pastry
blender or fork until mixture resembles small peas. Sprinkle
mixture evenly over batter in pans. Bake and cool as directed.

Lemon Tea Bread

makes 1 loaf
prep: 15 min. • **cook: 1 hr.**

1. Preheat oven to 350°. Beat softened butter at medium speed with an electric mixer until creamy. Gradually add 1 cup granulated sugar, beating until light and fluffy. Add eggs, 1 at a time, beating just until blended after each addition.

2. Stir together flour, baking powder, and salt; add to butter mixture alternately with milk, beating at low speed just until blended, beginning and ending with flour mixture. Stir in 1 Tbsp. lemon zest. Spoon batter into a greased and floured 8- x 4-inch loaf pan.

3. Bake at 350° for 1 hour or until a wooden pick inserted in center of bread comes out clean. Let cool in pan 10 minutes. Remove from pan to a wire rack, and cool completely.

4. Stir together powdered sugar and lemon juice until smooth; spoon over top of bread, letting excess drip down sides. Stir together remaining 1 Tbsp. lemon zest and 1 Tbsp. granulated sugar; sprinkle on top of bread.

Lemon-Almond Tea Bread: Stir ½ tsp. almond extract into batter. Proceed as directed.

½	cup butter, softened
1	cup granulated sugar
2	large eggs
1½	cups all-purpose flour
1	tsp. baking powder
½	tsp. salt
½	cup milk
2	Tbsp. lemon zest, divided
1	cup powdered sugar
2	Tbsp. fresh lemon juice
1	Tbsp. granulated sugar

Chocolate Bread

makes 2 loaves
prep: 21 min. • **cook: 25 min.** • **other: 3 hr., 15 min.**

1¼ cups warm milk (100° to 110°)

½ cup warm water (100° to 110°)

1 (¼-oz.) envelope active dry yeast

4½ cups all-purpose flour, divided

½ cup unsweetened cocoa

¼ cup granulated sugar

1 tsp. salt

1 large egg

2 Tbsp. butter, softened

2 (4-oz.) semisweet chocolate bars, chopped

1½ Tbsp. turbinado sugar

1. Combine milk, ½ cup warm water, and yeast in a large bowl; whisk until smooth. Let stand 5 minutes. Stir 2 cups flour, cocoa, granulated sugar, and salt into yeast mixture; beat at medium speed with an electric mixer until smooth. Beat in egg, butter, and 2 cups flour until a soft dough forms.

2. Turn out dough onto a floured surface, and knead until smooth (about 6 minutes), adding remaining ½ cup flour, 1 Tbsp. at a time as needed, to prevent dough from sticking. Fold in chopped chocolate during last minute of kneading.

3. Place dough in a large, lightly greased bowl, turning to coat top. Cover with plastic wrap, and let rise in a warm place (85°), free from drafts, 1 hour and 40 minutes or until doubled in bulk.

4. Punch dough down. Divide dough in half; gently shape each portion into an 8- x 4-inch oval. Place dough in 2 lightly greased 8½- x 4½-inch loaf pans. Cover and let rise 1½ hours or until doubled in bulk.

5. Preheat oven to 375°. Sprinkle loaves with turbinado sugar. Bake at 375° for 25 minutes or until loaves sound hollow when tapped. Remove from pans to wire racks, and let cool.

Note: We tested with Ghirardelli chocolate bars.

Fold/knead chopped chocolate into bread dough.

Place dough in loaf pans to rise.

Apricot-Almond Coffee Cake

makes 15 servings
prep: 20 min. • **cook: 25 min.** • **other: 20 min.**

4   oz. cream cheese, softened
½   cup apricot preserves
1   (16-oz.) package pound cake mix,
     divided
1   (8-oz.) container sour cream
½   cup milk
2   large eggs
½   tsp. almond extract
½   cup sliced almonds
Glaze

1. Preheat oven to 350°. Beat cream cheese, apricot preserves, and 1 Tbsp. cake mix at medium-low speed with an electric mixer just until blended.

2. Beat sour cream, milk, eggs, almond extract, and remaining cake mix at low speed 30 seconds or until blended. Increase speed to medium, and beat 3 more minutes.

3. Pour sour cream batter into a lightly greased 13- x 9-inch pan. Dollop cream cheese mixture by rounded tablespoonfuls evenly over batter. Swirl batter gently with a knife. Sprinkle almonds over top.

4. Bake at 350° for 25 to 30 minutes or until light golden and a wooden pick inserted in center comes out clean. Let cool in pan on a wire rack 20 minutes. Drizzle Glaze over slightly warm cake or individual pieces.

Note: We tested with Betty Crocker Pound Cake Mix.

Glaze:

makes ⅓ cup
prep: 5 min.

1   cup powdered sugar
½   tsp. vanilla extract
1   to 2 Tbsp. milk

1. Stir together powdered sugar, vanilla, and 1 Tbsp. milk in a small bowl until smooth. Stir in up to 1 Tbsp. additional milk, if necessary, for desired consistency.

Bananas Foster Upside-Down Coffee Cake

makes 8 to 10 servings
prep: 25 min. • **cook: 53 min.** • **other: 10 min.**

1. Preheat oven to 350°. Bake chopped pecans in a single layer in a shallow pan 8 to 10 minutes or until toasted and fragrant, stirring after 5 minutes.

2. Melt ¼ cup butter in a 10-inch cast-iron skillet over low heat; stir in rum. Sprinkle brown sugar over rum mixture. Remove from heat.

3. Sprinkle pecans evenly over brown sugar mixture. Cut bananas in half crosswise; cut each half lengthwise into 3 slices. Arrange banana slices in a spoke pattern over pecans. Cut 6 maraschino cherries in half. Place 1 cherry half between each banana slice. Place remaining whole cherry in center of skillet.

4. Beat remaining ¼ cup butter and ½ cup granulated sugar at medium speed with an electric mixer until blended. Add egg yolks, 1 at a time, beating just until blended after each addition. Add milk, sour cream, and vanilla, beating just until blended.

5. Combine baking mix and cinnamon. Add cinnamon mixture to sour cream mixture, beating just until blended.

6. Beat egg whites at high speed until soft peaks form. Gradually beat in remaining ¼ cup granulated sugar until stiff peaks form. Fold into batter. Spread batter over bananas in skillet.

7. Bake at 350° for 45 to 50 minutes or until a wooden pick inserted in center comes out clean. Let cool in skillet on a wire rack 10 minutes. Invert cake onto a serving plate. Serve warm with whipped cream, if desired.

Note: We tested with Bisquick Original Pancake and Baking Mix.

½ cup chopped pecans
½ cup butter, softened and divided
2 Tbsp. rum
1 cup firmly packed light brown sugar
2 medium-size ripe bananas
7 maraschino cherries
¾ cup granulated sugar, divided
2 large eggs, separated
¾ cup milk
½ cup sour cream
1 tsp. vanilla extract
2 cups all-purpose baking mix
¼ tsp. ground cinnamon
Whipped cream (optional)

Blackberry-Peach Coffee Cake

makes 8 servings
prep: 20 min. • **cook: 1 hr., 10 min.**

Streusel Topping
½   cup butter, softened
1   cup granulated sugar
2   large eggs
2   cups all-purpose flour
2   tsp. baking powder
½   tsp. salt
⅔   cup milk
2   tsp. vanilla extract
2   cups sliced and peeled fresh
     firm, ripe peaches (about 2 large
     peaches, 7 oz. each)
1   cup fresh blackberries
Powdered sugar
Garnishes: fresh blackberries, sliced
     peaches

1. Preheat oven to 350°. Prepare Streusel Topping.

2. Beat butter at medium speed with an electric mixer until creamy; gradually add granulated sugar, beating well. Add eggs, 1 at a time, beating until blended after each addition.

3. Combine flour, baking powder, and salt; add to butter mixture alternately with milk, beginning and ending with flour mixture. Beat at low speed until blended after each addition. Stir in vanilla. Pour batter into a greased and floured 9-inch springform pan; top with sliced peaches and blackberries. Pinch off 1-inch pieces of Streusel Topping, and drop over fruit.

4. Bake at 350° for 1 hour and 10 minutes to 1 hour and 20 minutes or until center of cake is set. (A wooden pick inserted in center will not come out clean.) Let cool completely on a wire rack (about 1½ hours). Dust with powdered sugar. Garnish, if desired.

Note: We found that using a shiny or light-colored pan gave us the best results. If you have a dark pan, wrap the outside of the pan with heavy-duty aluminum foil to get a similar result.

Streusel Topping:

makes 1½ cups
prep: 10 min.

½   cup butter, softened
½   cup granulated sugar
½   cup firmly packed light brown
     sugar
⅔   cup all-purpose flour
1   tsp. ground cinnamon
½   tsp. ground nutmeg

1. Beat butter at medium speed with an electric mixer until creamy; gradually add granulated sugar and brown sugar, beating well. Add flour, cinnamon, and nutmeg; beat just until blended.

Peach Coffee Cake: Omit blackberries. Increase peaches to 3 cups sliced (about 3 large peaches, 7 oz. each). Proceed with recipe as directed.

The American tradition of serving coffee and sweet cake along with gossip actually evolved from the tradition of English tea. This moist blueberry cream cheese cake with a lemon-sugar topping is special enough for company.

Blueberry 'n' Cheese Coffee Cake

makes 16 servings
prep: 11 min. • **cook: 50 min.**

½   cup butter, softened
1 ¼ cups sugar
2   large eggs
2   cups all-purpose flour
1   tsp. baking powder
1   tsp. salt
¾   cup milk
2   cups fresh blueberries
1   (8-oz.) package cream cheese, cut into ¼-inch cubes
½   cup all-purpose flour
½   cup sugar
2   Tbsp. lemon zest
2   Tbsp. butter, softened

1. Preheat oven to 375°. Beat ½ cup butter at medium speed with an electric mixer until creamy; gradually add 1¼ cups sugar, beating well. Add eggs, 1 at a time, beating until blended after each addition.

2. Combine 2 cups flour, baking powder, and salt; stir well. Combine milk and ¼ cup water; stir well. Add flour mixture to butter mixture alternately with milk mixture, beginning and ending with flour mixture. Mix at low speed after each addition until mixture is blended. Gently stir in blueberries and cream cheese. Pour batter into a greased 9-inch square pan.

3. Combine ½ cup flour and remaining 3 ingredients; stir well with a fork. Sprinkle mixture over batter. Bake at 375° for 50 to 55 minutes or until golden. Serve warm, or let cool completely on a wire rack.

tip:

If you find it difficult to cut the cream cheese into such small cubes, place it in the freezer for 20 minutes. But don't freeze it longer because partially frozen cream cheese will crumble.

Chocolate-Cream Cheese Coffee Cake

chocolate decadence

makes 24 servings
prep: 30 min. • cook: 45 min.

1. Preheat oven to 350°. Stir together 1⅓ cups flour and brown sugar in a small bowl. Cut butter into flour mixture with a pastry blender or fork until crumbly; stir in pecans. Set aside.

2. Beat cream cheese at medium speed with an electric mixer until smooth; add granulated sugar and 1 Tbsp. flour, beating until blended. Add egg and ½ tsp. vanilla, beating until blended.

3. Spoon Chocolate Velvet Cake Batter evenly into 2 greased and floured 9-inch springform pans. Dollop cream cheese mixture evenly over cake batter, and gently swirl through cake batter with a knife. Sprinkle reserved pecan mixture evenly over cake batter.

4. Bake at 350° for 45 minutes or until set. Let cool on a wire rack.

5. Whisk together powdered sugar, milk, and remaining ½ tsp. vanilla. Drizzle evenly over tops of coffee cakes.

1⅓ cups all-purpose flour
½ cup firmly packed brown sugar
½ cup cold butter, cut up
1 cup chopped pecans
1 (8-oz.) package cream cheese, softened
¼ cup granulated sugar
1 Tbsp. flour
1 large egg
1 tsp. vanilla extract, divided
Chocolate Velvet Cake Batter
1 cup powdered sugar
2 Tbsp. milk

Chocolate Velvet Cake Batter:

makes about 8½ cups
prep: 15 min.

1. Melt semisweet chocolate morsels in a microwave-safe bowl at HIGH for 30-second intervals until melted (about 1½ minutes total time). Stir until smooth.

2. Beat butter and brown sugar at medium speed with an electric mixer, beating about 5 minutes or until well blended. Add eggs, 1 at a time, beating just until blended after each addition. Add melted chocolate, beating just until blended.

3. Sift together flour, baking soda, and salt. Gradually add to chocolate mixture alternately with sour cream, beginning and ending with flour mixture. Beat at low speed just until blended after each addition. Gradually add 1 cup hot water in a slow, steady stream, beating at low speed just until blended. Stir in vanilla. Use immediately.

1½ cups semisweet chocolate morsels
½ cup butter, softened
1 (16-oz.) package light brown sugar
3 large eggs
2 cups all-purpose flour
1 tsp. baking soda
½ tsp. salt
1 (8-oz.) container sour cream
1 cup hot water
2 tsp. vanilla extract

Triple-Chocolate Coffee Cake

If you add the white chocolate drizzled on top to the three types of dark chocolate in this decadent treat, that's actually four chocolates in this recipe. What's not to love here?

makes 2 coffee cakes
prep: 15 min. • **cook: 25 min.**

1 (18.25-oz.) package devil's food cake mix
1 (3.9-oz.) package chocolate instant pudding mix
2 cups sour cream
1 cup butter, softened
5 large eggs
1 tsp. vanilla extract
3 cups semisweet chocolate morsels, divided
1 cup white chocolate morsels
1 cup chopped pecans, toasted

1. Preheat oven to 350°. Beat first 6 ingredients at low speed with an electric mixer 30 seconds or just until moistened; beat at medium speed 2 minutes. Stir in 2 cups semisweet chocolate morsels; pour batter evenly into 2 greased and floured 9-inch square cake pans.

2. Bake at 350° for 25 to 30 minutes or until a wooden pick inserted in center comes out clean. Let cool completely in pans on wire racks.

3. Microwave white chocolate morsels in a glass bowl at HIGH 30 to 60 seconds or until morsels melt, stirring at 30-second intervals until smooth. Drizzle evenly over cakes; repeat procedure with remaining 1 cup semisweet morsels. Sprinkle pecans over cakes. Cut into squares or wedges.

Streusel-Spiced Coffee Cake

holiday favorite

makes 12 servings
prep: 16 min. • **cook: 35 min.** • **other: 8 hr.**

1. Beat butter at medium speed with an electric mixer until fluffy; gradually add granulated sugar, beating well. Add eggs, 1 at a time, beating until blended after each addition. Add sour cream, mixing well.

2. Combine flour and next 5 ingredients; add to butter mixture, beating well. Spread batter into a greased and floured 13- x 9-inch pan.

3. Combine brown sugar, pecans, ½ tsp. cinnamon, and ¼ to ½ tsp. nutmeg in a small bowl. Sprinkle evenly over batter. Cover and refrigerate 8 hours.

4. Preheat oven to 350°. Remove pan from refrigerator and uncover; bake at 350° for 35 minutes or until a wooden pick inserted in center comes out clean.

¾	cup unsalted butter, softened
1	cup granulated sugar
2	large eggs
1	cup sour cream
2	cups all-purpose flour
2	tsp. baking powder
1	tsp. baking soda
½	tsp. ground cinnamon
½	tsp. grated nutmeg
½	tsp. salt
¾	cup firmly packed light brown sugar
1	cup coarsely chopped pecans
½	tsp. ground cinnamon
¼	to ½ tsp. grated nutmeg

Brown Sugar-Pecan Coffee Cake

makes 12 servings
prep: 20 min. • cook: 25 min. • other: 30 min.

2	cups all-purpose flour
2	cups firmly packed light brown sugar
¾	cup butter, cubed
1	cup sour cream
1	large egg, lightly beaten
1	tsp. baking soda
3	Tbsp. granulated sugar
1	tsp. ground cinnamon
1	cup chopped pecans

1. Preheat oven to 350°. Stir together flour and brown sugar in a large bowl. Cut ¾ cup butter into flour mixture with a pastry blender or 2 forks until crumbly. Press 2¾ cups crumb mixture evenly on the bottom of a lightly greased 13- x 9-inch pan.

2. Stir together sour cream, egg, and baking soda; add to remaining crumb mixture, stirring just until dry ingredients are moistened. Stir together granulated sugar and cinnamon. Pour sour cream mixture over crumb crust in pan; sprinkle evenly with cinnamon mixture and pecans.

3. Bake at 350° for 25 to 30 minutes or until a wooden pick inserted in center comes out clean. Let cool in pan on a wire rack 30 minutes. Serve warm.

Orange Coffee Rolls

makes 2 dozen
prep: 40 min. • **cook: 25 min.** • **other: 2 hr., 20 min.**

1. Combine yeast and warm water in a large mixing bowl; let stand 5 minutes. Add ¼ cup sugar and next 4 ingredients; beat at medium speed with an electric mixer until blended. Gradually stir in enough flour to make a soft dough.

2. Turn dough out onto a well-floured surface, and knead until smooth and elastic (about 5 minutes). Place in a well-greased bowl, turning to grease top. Cover and let rise in a warm place (85°), free from drafts, 1½ hours or until doubled in bulk.

3. Punch dough down, and divide in half. Roll 1 portion of dough into a 12-inch circle; brush with 1 Tbsp. melted butter. Combine remaining ¾ cup sugar, ¾ cup coconut, and orange zest; sprinkle half of coconut mixture over dough. Cut into 12 wedges; roll up each wedge, beginning at wide end. Place in a greased 13- x 9-inch pan, point side down. Repeat with remaining dough, butter, and coconut mixture.

4. Cover and let rise in a warm place, free from drafts, 45 minutes or until doubled in bulk. Preheat oven to 350°.

5. Bake at 350° for 25 to 30 minutes or until golden. (Cover with aluminum foil after 15 minutes to prevent excessive browning, if necessary.) Spoon warm Orange Glaze over warm rolls; sprinkle with remaining ¼ cup coconut.

Orange Glaze:

makes 1⅓ cups
prep: 5 min. • **cook: 5 min.**

1. Combine all ingredients in a small saucepan; bring to a boil. Boil 3 minutes, stirring occasionally. Let cool slightly.

tip:
If the dough is too elastic as you are rolling it in Step 3, stop, cover the dough, and let it rest for about 5 minutes. This allows the gluten to relax, making the dough easier to handle.

1	(¼-oz.) envelope active dry yeast
¼	cup warm water (100° to 110°)
1	cup sugar, divided
2	large eggs
½	cup sour cream
¼	cup plus 2 Tbsp. butter, melted
1	tsp. salt
2 ¾ to 3 cups all-purpose flour
2	Tbsp. butter, melted and divided
1	cup flaked coconut, toasted and divided
2	Tbsp. grated orange zest
Orange Glaze	

¾	cup sugar
½	cup sour cream
¼	cup butter
2	tsp. orange juice

King Cake has been a New Orleans tradition dating back to the 1800s. A coin, bean, or tiny plastic baby pressed into the risen dough before baking is said to bring the recipient good luck and once determined the Mardi Gras queen. Colored sugar toppings in the traditional colors of purple, green, and gold stand for justice, faith, and power.

King Cake

makes 18 servings
prep: 50 min. • **cook: 18 min.** • **other: 1 hr., 10 min.**

4 ¾ cups all-purpose flour, divided
1 cup granulated sugar, divided
1 ½ tsp. salt
2 (¼-oz.) envelopes rapid-rise yeast
¾ cup butter, divided
¾ cup milk
2 large eggs
1 Tbsp. ground cinnamon
2 cups sifted powdered sugar
3 Tbsp. milk
Colored sugars

1. Combine 1½ cups flour, ¼ cup sugar, salt, and yeast in a large bowl.

2. Melt ½ cup butter in a small saucepan over low heat. Add ¾ cup milk and ½ cup water, and heat until hot (120° to 130°). Add milk mixture to flour mixture, and beat at medium speed with an electric mixer 2 minutes. Add eggs, beating well. Stir in remaining 3¼ cups flour. Turn dough out onto a well-floured surface, and knead until smooth and elastic (about 10 minutes).

3. Place dough in a well-greased bowl, turning to grease top. Cover and let rise in a warm place (85°), free from drafts, 45 minutes or until doubled in bulk.

4. Stir together remaining ¾ cup sugar and cinnamon.

5. Preheat oven to 375°. Punch dough down, and let dough rest 6 minutes. Divide dough into 3 portions. Roll each portion into a 28- x 4-inch rectangle. Melt remaining ¼ cup butter; brush evenly over rectangles. Sprinkle each rectangle with ¼ cup sugar mixture, leaving a 1-inch margin around edges.

6. Roll up each dough rectangle, jelly-roll fashion, starting at 1 long side; pinch edges together to seal. Pinch ropes together at 1 end to seal, and braid. Cover and let rise in a warm place (85°), free from drafts, 15 minutes or until doubled in bulk.

7. Bake at 375° for 18 to 20 minutes or until golden. Transfer to a wire rack to cool completely.

8. Combine powdered sugar and 3 Tbsp. milk in a small bowl, stirring until smooth. Drizzle over cake, and sprinkle with colored sugars.

Commonly called "monkey bread," pull-apart bread is a variation on the sweet, buttery cinnamon rolls that ancient Middle Eastern cooks made. Their recipes traveled to Europe in the Middle Ages. While the technique varied according to culture and cuisine, the concept remained the same. Monkey bread became popular in the 1980s, presumably because Nancy Reagan served it at the White House.

Caramel-Nut Pull-Apart Bread

makes 12 servings
prep: 12 min. • **cook: 30 min.**

1. Preheat oven to 350°. Combine brown sugar and walnuts in a small bowl. Stir in butter. Spoon half of brown sugar mixture in bottom of a greased 12-cup Bundt pan.

2. Cut each biscuit in half (use kitchen scissors for quick cutting), and place in a large bowl. Sprinkle biscuits with cinnamon sugar; toss well to coat. Arrange half of biscuits over brown sugar mixture in Bundt pan. Spoon remaining brown sugar mixture over biscuits in pan; top with remaining biscuits.

3. Bake at 350° for 30 to 35 minutes or until browned. Turn out onto a serving platter immediately, spooning any remaining sauce over bread. Serve warm.

Note: We tested with Pillsbury Golden Layers Flaky Biscuits.

1   cup plus 2 Tbsp. firmly packed
    brown sugar
1   cup chopped walnuts
¾   cup butter, melted
3   (12-oz.) cans refrigerated biscuits
2   Tbsp. cinnamon sugar

Chocolate Chunk Scones

Serve these big chocolate wedges for breakfast or brunch with coffee, or for dessert with a dollop of whipped cream.

makes 1 dozen
prep: 25 min. • **cook: 36 min.**

4 cups all-purpose flour
⅔ cup sugar
½ cup unsweetened cocoa
4 tsp. baking powder
1½ tsp. baking soda
1 tsp. salt
½ tsp. freshly grated nutmeg
¾ cup cold butter, cut up
1 (11.5-oz.) package semisweet chocolate chunks
1 cup coarsely chopped walnuts or pecans (optional)
1¾ cups buttermilk
1 large egg, lightly beaten
2 tsp. vanilla extract
Parchment paper
2 Tbsp. sugar

1. Preheat oven to 350°. Whisk together flour and next 6 ingredients in a large bowl.

2. Cut butter into flour mixture with a pastry blender or fork until mixture is crumbly. Stir in chocolate chunks and, if desired, nuts.

3. Combine buttermilk, egg, and vanilla. Pour over crumb mixture; stir just until dry ingredients are moistened.

4. Turn dough out onto a lightly floured surface, and gently knead 3 or 4 times.

5. Divide dough in half; shape each half into a ball. Pat each into a 6-inch circle on parchment paper-lined baking sheets. Cut each circle into 6 wedges using a sharp knife (do not separate wedges). Sprinkle 2 Tbsp. sugar over dough.

6. Bake at 350° for 36 minutes or until a wooden pick inserted in center comes out clean. Separate into wedges. Serve warm, or remove to a wire rack to cool. Reheat scones in microwave at HIGH 20 to 25 seconds each.

Ginger Scones

Scottish scones are typically wedge-shaped, like these, flavored with crystallized ginger. Top the scones with sweetened whipped cream, if desired.

makes 8 scones
prep: 20 min. • **cook: 18 min.**

1. Preheat oven to 400°. Combine first 4 ingredients in a large bowl; cut butter into flour mixture with a pastry blender until crumbly. Stir in ginger. Add milk, stirring just until dry ingredients are moistened. Turn dough out onto a lightly floured surface, and knead 10 to 15 times. Pat or roll dough to ¾-inch thickness; shape into a round, and cut dough into 8 wedges. Place wedges on a lightly greased baking sheet.

2. Bake at 400° for 18 to 22 minutes or until scones are barely golden. Cool slightly on a wire rack. Serve warm.

2 ¾	cups all-purpose flour
2	tsp. baking powder
½	tsp. salt
½	cup sugar
¾	cup butter, cut up
⅓	cup chopped crystallized ginger
1	cup milk

tip:

Crystallized ginger has been cooked in a sugar syrup and coated with sugar. Before you begin to chop the ginger, coat the knife blade with vegetable cooking spray to prevent the task from becoming unmanageably sticky.

Cacao and Milk Chocolate Scones

This recipe is like a sweet version of drop biscuits. Find cacao nibs packaged at gourmet food stores.

makes 14 scones
prep: 12 min. • **cook: 18 min.**

3	cups all-purpose flour
⅔	cup granulated sugar
1	Tbsp. baking powder
½	tsp. salt
¾	cup cold unsalted butter, cut into pieces
1	cup milk chocolate morsels or chopped milk chocolate bar
½	cup cacao nibs or chopped toasted pecans
1	large egg
1	cup whipping cream
2	tsp. vanilla extract

Parchment paper
Whipping cream (optional)
Coarse or granulated sugar (optional)

1. Preheat oven to 425°. Stir together first 4 ingredients in a large bowl; cut in butter with a pastry blender until crumbly. Stir in chocolate morsels and cacao nibs.

2. Whisk together egg, 1 cup whipping cream, and vanilla; add to flour mixture, stirring with a fork just until dry ingredients are moistened and mixture forms a shaggy dough. Using a ⅓-cup measuring cup, scoop dough into mounds onto parchment paper-lined baking sheets. Brush scones with additional cream, and sprinkle with sugar, if desired.

3. Bake at 425° for 18 minutes or until golden. Serve warm.

Note: We tested with Hershey's milk chocolate bar.

Cacao nibs are unsweetened, roasted, and crushed cacao beans. They give these scones a toasty, bittersweet flavor.

Brush scones with cream; sprinkle with sugar for a crunchy finish.

Bread Puddings, Custards & More

We've stirred some all-time favorite flavor combinations into stellar desserts, like Best-Ever Banana Pudding and So-Easy Chocolate Soufflés. Whether casual or formal, your next gathering will be complete with one of these superb desserts. We think you'll agree—these luscious dishes are simply divine. So pick up a spoon and indulge.

Since when did anyone consider chocolate pudding a "health food?" While medical journals in today's world won't list any pudding recipes, the dessert has come a long way since its creation in the Middle Ages.

When you think of health food, it's doubtful that you picture a creamy bowl of pudding, but in the late 19th century, food companies portrayed pudding as nutritious, especially for children. The puddings of today closely match the custards of yesteryear. The culinary encyclopedia *Larousse Gastronomique* defines pudding as "Any of numerous dishes, sweet or savory, served hot or cold, which are prepared in a variety of ways." While this is a very broad description, cooks have always found new ways of enjoying the creamy dish.

Bread pudding evolved as a practical solution for salvaging day-old French bread that had become too hard for sandwiches. Often served with a whiskey-laced sauce, it's a signature dessert of New Orleans.

In the late 19th century, brands such as Jell-O and Royal began producing instant pudding mixes, complete with recipes printed on the packages. The American public ate up these new dishes beginning in the 1930s, thus solidifying pudding as a staple on the American dining table.

Whether you prefer Cherry Bread Pudding, Creamy Rice Pudding with Praline Sauce, or So-Easy Chocolate Soufflé, you'll realize with the first taste that puddings, custards, and soufflés are classic comfort foods.

Spiced Caramel-Apple Bread Pudding

makes 8 servings
prep: 20 min. • **cook: 47 min.** • **other: 1 hr.**

1   Granny Smith apple, peeled and
       chopped
½   tsp. ground cinnamon, divided
½   (16-oz.) Italian bread loaf,
       cut into bite-size pieces
Vegetable cooking spray
3   large eggs
1½   cups 2% reduced-fat milk
1   cup apple cider
¼   cup firmly packed brown sugar
1   tsp. vanilla extract
¼   tsp. ground nutmeg
Toasted Pecan-Caramel Sauce

1. Sauté apple and ¼ tsp. cinnamon in a lightly greased skillet over medium-high heat 2 minutes or until tender. Stir together bread and apple mixture in an 11- x 7-inch baking dish coated with cooking spray.

2. Whisk together eggs, milk, apple cider, brown sugar, vanilla, nutmeg, and remaining ¼ tsp. cinnamon; pour over bread mixture in baking dish. Cover and chill 1 hour.

3. Preheat oven to 350°. Bake bread mixture at 350° for 45 to 50 minutes or until top is crisp and golden brown. Serve warm with Toasted Pecan-Caramel Sauce.

Toasted Pecan-Caramel Sauce:

makes about ¾ cup
prep: 10 min. • **cook: 20 min.**

¼   cup chopped pecans
¾   cup sugar
1   tsp. light corn syrup
½   cup evaporated milk
1½   tsp. butter

1. Preheat oven to 350°. Bake pecans in a single layer in a shallow pan 8 to 10 minutes or until toasted and fragrant.

2. Sprinkle sugar in an even layer in a small saucepan. Stir together syrup and ⅓ cup water, and pour over sugar in saucepan. Cook, without stirring, over medium-high heat 12 to 14 minutes or until sugar is dissolved and mixture is golden.

3. Remove from heat. Gradually whisk in evaporated milk. (Mixture will bubble.) Stir in butter and toasted pecans.

Blueberry Bread Pudding

Make this easy, decadent recipe the day before, and chill; then bake and serve hot.

makes 10 to 12 servings
prep: 15 min. • cook: 1 hr. • other: 8 hr.

1 (16-oz.) French bread loaf, cubed
1 (8-oz.) package cream cheese, cut into pieces
3 cups fresh blueberries, divided
6 large eggs
4 cups milk
½ cup sugar
¼ cup butter, melted
¼ cup maple syrup
1 (10-oz.) jar blueberry preserves
Garnishes: fresh mint leaves, edible pansies

1. Arrange half of bread cubes in a lightly greased 13- x 9-inch pan. Sprinkle evenly with cream cheese and 1 cup blueberries; top with remaining bread cubes.

2. Whisk together eggs, 4 cups milk, sugar, butter, and maple syrup; pour over bread mixture, pressing bread cubes to absorb egg mixture. Cover and chill 8 hours.

3. Preheat oven to 350°. Bake, covered, at 350° for 30 minutes. Uncover and bake 30 more minutes or until lightly browned and set. Let stand 5 minutes before serving.

4. Stir together remaining 2 cups blueberries and blueberry preserves in a saucepan over low heat until warm. Serve blueberry mixture over bread pudding. Garnish, if desired.

Cherry Bread Pudding

As it bakes, bread pudding will rise to the tops of the ramekins and may overflow. It will deflate once it's removed from the oven.

makes 6 servings
prep: 25 min. • **cook: 30 min.** • **other: 40 min.**

1. Preheat oven to 350°. Place bread pieces in 6 (8-oz.) ramekins coated with cooking spray. Place ramekins on a baking sheet.

2. Whisk together milk and next 8 ingredients until blended. Pour milk mixture over bread in ramekins; let stand 30 minutes, pressing bread to absorb mixture after 15 minutes.

3. Bake at 350° for 30 to 35 minutes or just until a knife inserted in center comes out clean. Let stand 10 minutes. Spoon Cherry Sauce over bread pudding.

Note: We tested with Splenda No Calorie Sweetener, Granulated.

Cherry Sauce:

makes about 1 cup
prep: 5 min. • **cook: 16 min.**

1. Combine all ingredients in a small saucepan. Cook over medium-high heat, stirring occasionally, 16 to 18 minutes or until most of the liquid is reduced.

Note: We tested with Kirsch Cherry Liqueur.

tip:

Instead of ramekins, you can place bread pieces in an 11- x 7-inch baking dish coated with cooking spray, and proceed with the recipe as directed. (No need to place on a baking sheet.) Bake at 350° for 30 to 35 minutes or just until a knife inserted in center comes out clean. Let stand 10 minutes.

1	(8-oz.) French bread loaf, cut into 1-inch pieces
	Vegetable cooking spray
2	cups fat-free milk
½	(12-oz.) can evaporated fat-free milk
¾	cup no-calorie sweetener
¾	cup egg substitute
¼	cup sugar
1	Tbsp. butter, melted
1	tsp. vanilla extract
½	tsp. ground cinnamon
¼	tsp. ground nutmeg
	Cherry Sauce

1	(15-oz.) can pitted tart cherries in water
3	Tbsp. light brown sugar
2	Tbsp. cherry-flavored liqueur

Peanut Butter-Banana Sandwich Bread Puddings With Dark Caramel Sauce

These puff much like soufflés, so present them right out of the oven to your guests.

makes 8 servings
prep: 25 min. • **cook: 20 min.** • **other: 2 hr., 30 min.**

8	buttermilk bread slices, crusts removed
½	cup creamy peanut butter
2	bananas, thinly sliced
2	large eggs
½	cup granulated sugar
2	Tbsp. brown sugar
1 ¾	cups whipping cream

Peanut Butter Streusel Topping
Dark Caramel Sauce
Garnish: powdered sugar

1. Spread bread slices with peanut butter. Top 4 bread slices with bananas and remaining bread slices, peanut butter sides down, pressing firmly. Cut sandwiches into 1-inch pieces; place in 8 lightly greased (8-oz.) ramekins.

2. Whisk together eggs and sugars; whisk in whipping cream. Gradually pour mixture over sandwich pieces in ramekins; sprinkle with Peanut Butter Streusel Topping. Place ramekins in a 15- x 10-inch jelly-roll pan. Cover and chill 2 to 24 hours.

3. Preheat oven to 375°. Let puddings stand at room temperature 30 minutes. Bake at 375° for 20 to 25 minutes or until golden brown, set, and puffed. Serve warm with Dark Caramel Sauce. Garnish, if desired.

Note: We tested with Pepperidge Farm Buttermilk Farmhouse Soft Bread.

Peanut Butter Streusel Topping:

makes 1 cup
prep: 10 min.

¼	cup all-purpose flour
¼	cup firmly packed brown sugar
2	Tbsp. butter
2	Tbsp. creamy peanut butter
¼	cup chopped salted peanuts

1. Stir together flour and brown sugar in a bowl. Cut in butter and peanut butter with a pastry blender or fork until mixture resembles small peas. Stir in peanuts.

tip:
This bread pudding mixture may be prepared in an 11- x 7-inch baking dish. Bake at 375° for 35 minutes or until golden brown, set, and puffed.

Dark Caramel Sauce:

makes 1½ cups
prep: 16 min. • **cook: 11 min.** • **other: 15 min.**

1. Cook sugar in a 3-qt. heavy saucepan over medium heat 6 to 8 minutes or until sugar caramelizes, tilting and swirling pan to incorporate mixture. Stir in whipping cream. (Mixture will bubble and harden.) Cook, stirring constantly, until mixture melts and begins to boil (about 5 minutes). Quickly pour sauce into a bowl; stir in vanilla and salt. Let cool 15 minutes. Serve warm or cool.

Note: To make ahead, cover and chill up to 3 weeks. To reheat, cook, uncovered, in a microwave-safe glass bowl at MEDIUM LOW (30% power) for 2 minutes or until warm, stirring once.

1 cup sugar
1 cup whipping cream
1 tsp. vanilla extract
⅛ to ¼ tsp. salt

bread puddings, custards & more

Caramel-Pecan-Pumpkin Bread Puddings

makes 11 servings
prep: 27 min. • **bake: 55 min.** • **other: 8 hr.**

1. Whisk together eggs and next 8 ingredients in a large bowl until well blended. Add bread pieces, stirring to coat thoroughly. Cover with plastic wrap, and chill 8 to 24 hours.

2. Preheat oven to 350°. Spoon bread mixture into 11 (6-oz.) lightly greased ramekins. (Ramekins will be completely full, and mixture will mound slightly.) Place ramekins on an aluminum foil-lined jelly-roll pan.

3. Bake at 350° for 50 minutes, shielding with foil after 30 minutes.

4. Remove bread puddings from oven; drizzle with Caramel-Pecan Sauce. Bake 5 minutes or until sauce is thoroughly heated and begins to bubble.

Caramel-Pecan Sauce:

1. During last 15 minutes of baking bread puddings, prepare Caramel-Pecan Sauce: Heat pecans in a medium skillet over medium-low heat, stirring often, 3 to 5 minutes or until lightly toasted and fragrant.

2. Cook brown sugar, butter, and corn syrup in a small saucepan over medium heat, stirring occasionally, 3 to 4 minutes or until sugar is dissolved. Remove from heat; stir in vanilla and pecans.

One-Dish Caramel-Pecan-Pumpkin Bread Pudding: Prepare recipe as directed in Step 1. Spoon chilled bread mixture into a lightly greased 13- x 9-inch baking dish. Cover with aluminum foil. Bake, covered, at 350° for 35 minutes. Uncover and bake 15 minutes. Prepare Caramel-Pecan Sauce as directed. Proceed with recipe as directed in Step 4.

4	large eggs
2	(15-oz.) cans pumpkin
1½	cups milk
1	cup half-and-half
1	cup sugar
1	tsp. ground cinnamon
½	tsp. salt
½	tsp. ground nutmeg
½	tsp. vanilla extract
1	(12-oz.) French bread loaf, cut into 1-inch pieces (about 10 cups)

Caramel-Pecan Sauce

1	cup pecans, chopped
1	cup firmly packed light brown sugar
½	cup butter
1	Tbsp. light corn syrup
1	tsp. vanilla extract

Stuffed Pumpkin With Cranberry-Raisin Bread Pudding

makes 12 servings
prep: 10 min. • cook: 1 hr.

1	(2½- to 3-lb.) pumpkin (see Note)
2	Tbsp. butter, melted and divided
2	Tbsp. sugar, divided
2	large eggs
½	cup sugar
½	cup butter, melted
¾	cup half-and-half
¾	cup chopped pecans, toasted
1	(16-oz.) raisin bread loaf, cut into 1-inch cubes
½	cup fresh cranberries
	Lemon-Vanilla Sauce

1. Preheat oven to 350°. Cut off top of pumpkin, reserving lid with stem. Scoop out pumpkin seeds and pulp, and reserve for another use. Brush inside of pumpkin shell with 1 Tbsp. melted butter. Sprinkle with 1 Tbsp. sugar. Top with lid.

2. Bake at 350° for 35 minutes.

3. Brush inside of baked pumpkin shell with 1 Tbsp. butter; sprinkle with 1 Tbsp. sugar.

4. Stir together eggs and next 6 ingredients; spoon pudding mixture into a lightly greased 8-inch square pan.

5. Bake pumpkin and bread pudding at 350° for 25 minutes. Let pumpkin cool; spoon bread pudding evenly into pumpkin shell. Serve with Lemon-Vanilla Sauce.

Note: For individual servings, substitute 12 (½-lb.) pumpkins. Scoop out seeds and pulp; sprinkle each pumpkin shell with 1 tsp. butter and 1 tsp. sugar, and bake with the bread pudding. (Do not prebake as with the larger pumpkin.) Spoon bread pudding evenly into baked pumpkin shells.

Lemon-Vanilla Sauce:

makes 1⅔ cups

1	vanilla bean, split
½	cup sugar
2	Tbsp. cornstarch
⅛	tsp. salt
1	Tbsp. butter
2	Tbsp. lemon zest
⅓	cup fresh lemon juice

1. Cook vanilla bean, 1 cup water, sugar, cornstarch, and salt in a saucepan over medium heat, stirring until smooth and thickened.

2. Stir in butter and remaining ingredients, and cook until thoroughly heated. Remove vanilla bean.

In the hundreds of versions of this classic dessert, sweeteners vary from sugar to molasses, and breads from biscuits to French bread. Stale bread is the one factor they all have in common.

Brown Sugar Bread Pudding With Crème Anglaise

makes 9 servings
prep: 30 min. • **cook: 30 min.** • **other: 10 min.**

1. Preheat oven to 350°. Whisk together egg whites and egg in a medium bowl until blended. Whisk in reduced-fat milk and next 7 ingredients.

2. Arrange bread cubes in an 8-inch square pan coated with cooking spray. Pour egg mixture evenly over bread. Sprinkle evenly with 4 tsp. brown sugar, butter, and almonds. Press down gently on bread cubes, and let stand 10 minutes.

3. Bake at 350° for 30 to 35 minutes or until a knife inserted in center comes out clean. Serve warm with 2 Tbsp. chilled Crème Anglaise per serving.

Crème Anglaise:

makes 2⅔ cups
prep: 10 min. • **cook: 15 min.**

1. Cut a 2-inch piece of vanilla bean, and split lengthwise. Reserve remaining bean for other uses. Combine vanilla bean, whipping cream, and milk in a medium-size heavy saucepan. Cook over medium heat, stirring constantly, until mixture reaches 185°.

2. Combine yolks and sugar in a bowl; beat with a wire whisk until blended. Gradually stir about one-fourth of hot mixture into yolks; add to remaining hot mixture, stirring constantly. Cook over low heat, stirring constantly, 6 minutes or until thickened. Discard vanilla bean, and stir in liqueur. Cover and chill.

4	egg whites
1	large egg
1¼	cups 2% reduced-fat milk
¾	cup evaporated fat-free milk
½	cup firmly packed light brown sugar
1	tsp. ground cinnamon
¼	tsp. ground nutmeg
⅛	tsp. salt
⅛	tsp. ground allspice
2	tsp. vanilla extract
1	(12-oz.) day-old French bread loaf, cut into 1-inch cubes (about 8 cups)
	Vegetable cooking spray
4	tsp. light brown sugar
½	Tbsp. butter, cut into small pieces
¼	cup sliced almonds, toasted
	Crème Anglaise

1	vanilla bean
1⅓	cups whipping cream
⅔	cup milk
4	egg yolks
½	cup sugar
½	cup Irish cream liqueur

Chocolate Bread Pudding With Chocolate Liqueur Cream

Chocolate liqueur and semisweet chocolate turn humble bread pudding made with slices of white bread into an uptown dessert fit for company. Whipped cream spiked with chocolate liqueur adds the crowning touch.

makes 6 servings
prep: 20 min. • **cook: 1 hr.** • **other: 15 min.**

5	cups diced white bread
1	cup semisweet chocolate morsels
3	cups milk
3	Tbsp. chocolate liqueur or crème de cacao
3	egg yolks
⅓	cup sugar
½	tsp. ground cinnamon
¼	tsp. salt
1	tsp. vanilla extract
1	cup whipping cream
2	Tbsp. chocolate liqueur or crème de cacao

Ground cinnamon

1. Preheat oven to 350°. Combine bread and chocolate morsels in a greased 11- x 7-inch baking dish. Stir together milk and next 6 ingredients; pour milk mixture over bread mixture. Let stand 15 minutes.

2. Bake at 350° for 1 hour or until puffy and set.

3. Beat whipping cream until foamy; gradually add 2 Tbsp. chocolate liqueur, beating until soft peaks form. Cut bread pudding into squares, top with whipped cream, and sprinkle with ground cinnamon.

tip:

If you're entertaining and want to do as much as possible ahead, spoon the beaten cream mixture in Step 3 into 6 mounds on a baking sheet lined with wax paper, and freeze up to 6 hours. Let thaw 3 minutes before placing on top of each serving.

Summer Pudding

This colorful pudding is best made in the summer when berries are at their best.

makes 4 servings
prep: 15 min. • **cook: 10 min.** • **other: 2 hr.**

1. Combine first 8 ingredients and, if desired, liqueur, lemon verbena, and peppercorns in a large nonaluminum bowl. Cover and let stand at room temperature at least 1½ hours.

2. Preheat oven to 350°. Spread bread cubes evenly on a baking sheet; bake at 350° for 10 to 15 minutes or until toasted. Let cool.

3. Stir bread into berry mixture, and let stand for 30 minutes. Remove and discard lemon verbena.

4. Spoon pudding mixture into 4 (8-oz.) individual serving dishes. Garnish, if desired.

Note: We tested with Sara Lee Honey White Bakery Bread.

2	cups fresh raspberries
1	cup fresh blackberries
1	cup quartered fresh strawberries
½	cup sugar
1	Tbsp. lemon zest
2	Tbsp. fresh lemon juice
½	tsp. vanilla extract
⅛	tsp. salt
2	Tbsp. raspberry or blackberry liqueur (optional)
1	lemon verbena sprig (optional)
½	tsp. crushed green peppercorns (optional)
2	cups day-old white bread slices, cut into ½-inch cubes

Garnishes: fresh blackberries, fresh blueberries, fresh strawberries

Pound Cake Banana Pudding

This recipe was inspired by the pudding served at the famous Mrs. Wilkes' Dining Room in Savannah, Georgia.

makes 10 to 12 servings
prep: 20 min. • cook: 28 min. • other: 6 hr.

1. Whisk together first 5 ingredients in a saucepan over medium-low heat; cook, whisking constantly, 13 to 15 minutes or until thickened. Remove from heat; stir in butter and vanilla until butter melts.

2. Layer half of pound cake cubes, half of bananas, and half of pudding mixture in a lightly greased 3-qt. round baking dish. Repeat layers. Cover pudding, and chill 6 hours.

3. Preheat oven to 375°. Prepare Vanilla Meringue, and spread over pudding. Bake at 375° for 15 minutes or until golden brown.

Note: We tested with Sara Lee Family Size All Butter Pound Cake.

4	cups half-and-half
4	egg yolks
1½	cups sugar
¼	cup cornstarch
¼	tsp. salt
3	Tbsp. butter
2	tsp. vanilla extract
1	(1-lb.) pound cake, cubed
4	large ripe bananas, sliced
	Vanilla Meringue

Vanilla Meringue:

makes about 3½ cups
prep: 10 min.

1. Combine sugar and salt.

2. Beat egg whites and vanilla at high speed with an electric mixer until foamy. Add sugar mixture, 1 Tbsp. at a time, and beat 2 to 3 minutes or until stiff peaks form and sugar dissolves.

¼	cup sugar
⅛	tsp. salt
4	egg whites
¼	tsp. vanilla extract

Best-Ever Banana Pudding

makes 12 to 14 servings
prep: 15 min. • **cook: 15 min.**

1. Combine first 3 ingredients in a large heavy saucepan. Whisk milk and egg yolks until blended; add to dry ingredients, whisking until smooth. Cook over medium heat, whisking constantly, 15 to 20 minutes or until thickened. Remove from heat; stir in vanilla.

2. Arrange one-third of vanilla wafers in bottom of a 4-qt. serving bowl. Slice 2 bananas; layer over wafers, and spoon one-third of custard over bananas. Repeat procedure twice.

3. Beat whipping cream at medium speed with an electric mixer until foamy; gradually add powdered sugar to mixture, beating until soft peaks form. Spread over custard. Garnish, if desired. Serve immediately, or cover and chill 8 hours.

2 ⅔ cups granulated sugar
½   cup all-purpose flour
⅛   tsp. salt
6   cups milk
6   egg yolks
2   tsp. vanilla extract
1   (12-oz.) package vanilla wafers
6   bananas
1 ½ cups whipping cream
¼   cup powdered sugar
Garnish: banana chips

tip:

For Individual Best-Ever Banana Puddings, prepare recipe as directed in Step 1. Slice bananas. Layer half each of vanilla wafers, custard, and bananas among 14 (8-oz.) ramekins. Repeat layers. Proceed with recipe as directed.

kids love it

Blastin' Banana-Blueberry Pudding

If you prefer a less sweet banana pudding, just omit the powdered sugar from the whipped cream.

makes 10 to 12 servings
prep: 10 min. • cook: 20 min. • other: 4 hr., 10 min.

4	cups milk
4	egg yolks
1½	cups granulated sugar
⅓	cup all-purpose flour
2	Tbsp. butter
1	Tbsp. vanilla extract
1	(12-oz.) box vanilla wafers
4	large ripe bananas, sliced
2	cups frozen blueberries
1½	cups whipping cream
3	Tbsp. powdered sugar

1. Whisk together first 4 ingredients in a large saucepan over medium-low heat. Cook, whisking constantly, 20 minutes or until thickened. Remove from heat; stir in butter and vanilla until butter melts. Let stand 10 minutes.

2. Arrange half of vanilla wafers evenly in a 13- x 9-inch baking dish; top with half of banana slices and half of blueberries. Spoon half of pudding mixture evenly over fruit. Repeat layers. Cover and chill 4 hours.

3. Beat whipping cream at high speed with an electric mixer until foamy; gradually add powdered sugar, beating until soft peaks form. Spread evenly over chilled pudding. Serve immediately.

bread puddings, custards & more

Creamy Rice Pudding With Praline Sauce

If you're a fan of pure and simple old-fashioned desserts, this dish is for you. The praline sauce takes it to the next level.

makes 6 to 8 servings
prep: 15 min. • cook: 50 min.

1. Stir together first 3 ingredients and 2 cups half-and-half in a large saucepan. Cover and cook over medium-low heat, stirring often, 35 to 40 minutes or until rice is tender.

2. Whisk together egg yolks, ½ cup half-and-half, and sugar. Gradually stir about one-fourth of hot rice mixture into yolk mixture; stir yolk mixture into remaining hot mixture. Cook over medium-low heat, stirring constantly, until mixture reaches 160° and is thickened and bubbly (about 7 minutes). Remove from heat; stir in vanilla.

3. Stir together caramels and remaining ¼ cup half-and-half in a small saucepan over medium-low heat until smooth. Stir in pecans. Serve praline sauce over rice pudding.

Note: We tested with Mahatma Rice.

2	cups milk
1	cup uncooked extra long-grain white rice
½	tsp. salt
2 ¾	cups half-and-half, divided
4	egg yolks, beaten
½	cup sugar
1 ½	tsp. vanilla extract
20	caramels
½	cup chopped toasted pecans

White Chocolate Rice Pudding With Dried Cherry Sauce

The seeds and pod of a vanilla bean simmer in this rich rice pudding. Be sure to stir it often so it doesn't scorch.

makes 8 servings
prep: 10 min. • **cook: 45 min.** • **other: 5 min.**

1 ½	cups hot water
¾	cup medium-grain rice
1	vanilla bean, split lengthwise
½	cup sugar
4	cups half-and-half
¼	tsp. salt
¾	cup white chocolate morsels
Dried Cherry Sauce	
½	cup sliced almonds, toasted

1. Combine water and rice in a large saucepan. Bring to a boil. Cover, reduce heat, and simmer 15 minutes or until liquid is absorbed and rice is tender.

2. Scrape seeds from vanilla bean into pan. Stir seeds, pod, sugar, half-and-half, and salt into rice. Cook over medium-low heat 30 minutes, stirring often. Remove vanilla bean pod. Add white chocolate morsels, stirring until melted. Let cool 5 minutes. Spoon rice pudding into 8 individual serving dishes. If not serving immediately, cover and chill. When ready to serve, top with Dried Cherry Sauce, and sprinkle with almonds.

Dried Cherry Sauce:

makes 1 cup
prep: 6 min. • **cook: 27 min.**

½	cup dried cherries or cranberries
2	cups Merlot
¾	cup sugar
1	tsp. orange zest
1	tsp. grated fresh ginger

1. Combine all ingredients in a medium saucepan. Bring to a boil; reduce heat, and cook, uncovered, 27 minutes or until sauce coats a spoon and is reduced to 1 cup, stirring occasionally. Cool completely.

Ultimate Chocolate Pudding

Definitive in flavor and silky in texture, this pudding deserves a place in the chocolate hall of fame.

makes 3½ cups
prep: 10 min. • **cook: 10 min.** • **other: 10 min.**

1. Whisk together first 4 ingredients in a medium saucepan. Gradually whisk in milk. Cook over medium heat, stirring constantly, until pudding boils and is thickened (about 8 to 10 minutes). Reduce heat to medium–low, and cook 2 more minutes. Remove from heat; add butter and vanilla, stirring gently until butter melts. Place heavy-duty plastic wrap directly on warm pudding (to keep a film from forming); cool 10 minutes.

2. Serve warm, or chill until ready to serve. Top with whipped cream. Serve with cookies.

Note: For rich chocolate flavor, order double-Dutch dark cocoa online at www.kingarthurflour.com. We tested with Pepperidge Farm Milano cookies.

1 ¼ cups sugar
½ cup Dutch process cocoa
¼ cup cornstarch
½ tsp. salt
2 ½ cups milk
⅓ cup unsalted butter, cut up
2 tsp. vanilla extract
Unsweetened whipped cream
Chocolate-filled vanilla wafer
    sandwich cookies

Caramel Custard

The hot water bath helps insulate the custard from the direct heat of the oven and provides a more gentle environment for even baking.

makes 10 servings
prep: 5 min. • **cook: 1 hr., 5 min.** • **other: 3 hr., 5 min.**

½   cup sugar

2   egg yolks

1   large egg

1   (14-oz.) can fat-free sweetened condensed milk

1   (12-oz.) can evaporated fat-free milk

3   oz. ⅓-less-fat cream cheese, softened

1   Tbsp. vanilla extract

1. Preheat oven to 350°. Cook sugar in an 8-inch round cake pan (with 2-inch sides) over medium heat, shaking pan occasionally, 5 minutes or until sugar melts and turns light golden brown. Remove pan from heat, and let stand 5 minutes. (Sugar will harden.)

2. Process egg yolks and remaining ingredients in a blender until smooth. Pour mixture over caramelized sugar in pan. Cover mixture with aluminum foil.

3. Place cake pan in a broiler pan. Add hot water (150°) to pan to a depth of ⅔ inch.

4. Bake at 350° for 1 hour or until a knife inserted in center of custard comes out clean. Remove cake pan from water bath; cool completely on a wire rack. Cover and chill at least 3 hours.

5. Run a knife around edge of pan to loosen; invert onto a serving plate.

Banana-Caramel Custard: Prepare custard recipe as directed, adding 1 medium-size ripe banana to egg yolk mixture in blender.

tip:
The 8-oz. blocks of ⅓-less-fat cream cheese have marks on the packaging noting 1-oz. measurements. By using these marks, it's easy to measure the 3 oz. of cream cheese that you need for this recipe.

Café Con Leche Custard Cups

makes 8 servings
prep: 10 min. • cook: 10 min. • other: 30 min.

⅓   cup all-purpose flour

⅛   tsp. salt

2 ½ cups 2% reduced-fat milk

1   (14-oz.) can fat-free sweetened
     condensed milk

2   egg yolks

2   Tbsp. instant coffee granules

2   tsp. vanilla extract

¾   cup thawed reduced-fat whipped
     topping

Garnishes: chopped and whole
     chocolate-covered espresso
     beans

1. Combine flour and salt in a 2-qt. heavy nonaluminum sauce-pan. Whisk in reduced-fat milk and next 3 ingredients, whisking until smooth. Cook over medium heat, whisking constantly, 10 to 12 minutes or until thickened. Remove from heat; stir in vanilla.

2. Fill a large bowl with ice; place pan in ice, and whisk custard occasionally until completely cool (about 30 minutes).

3. Spoon ½ cup custard into each of 8 (5-oz.) cups or glasses. Top each with 1 to 2 Tbsp. whipped topping, filling completely. Scrape top with a knife to level whipped topping. Garnish, if desired.

tip:

To make ahead, pour cooled custard into a gallon-size zip-top plastic bag, gently pressing out excess air (to prevent a film from forming). Seal bag, and chill up to 24 hours.
To serve, snip off 1 corner of bag, and pipe custard into serving cups.

Spiced Soufflés With Lemon Whipped Cream

makes 8 servings
prep: 20 min. • **cook: 23 min.** • **other: 20 min.**

1. Grease bottom and sides of 8 (6-oz.) ramekins or custard cups evenly with butter. Lightly coat bottom and sides evenly with sugar, shaking out excess. Place ramekins in a 13- x 9-inch pan or baking dish. Set aside.

2. Melt ¼ cup butter in a small saucepan over medium heat; whisk in flour. Cook, whisking constantly, 1 minute. Gradually whisk in milk, whisking constantly until thickened. Remove from heat. Whisk in ⅔ cup sugar and next 5 ingredients.

3. Beat egg yolks at high speed with an electric mixer 4 to 5 minutes or until thick and pale. Gradually whisk about one-fourth of hot mixture into yolks; add to remaining hot mixture, whisking constantly. Cook over medium heat 1 minute. Remove from heat; let stand 20 minutes.

4. Preheat oven to 400°. Beat egg whites at high speed with an electric mixer until soft peaks form. Gently fold egg whites into milk mixture. Spoon evenly into each ramekin, filling to top.

5. Bake at 400° for 18 to 20 minutes or until puffed and set. Serve immediately with Lemon Whipped Cream.

Lemon Whipped Cream:

This is also fabulous with fresh berries in the spring.

makes 2 cups
prep: 5 min.

1. Beat whipping cream at high speed with an electric mixer until foamy; gradually add sugar, lemon zest, and lemon juice, beating until soft peaks form.

Butter, softened
Sugar
¼	cup butter
¼	cup all-purpose flour
1 ¼	cups milk
⅔	cup sugar
¼	cup molasses
2	tsp. ground ginger
1	tsp. ground cinnamon
¼	tsp. salt
1	tsp. vanilla extract
5	large eggs, separated

Lemon Whipped Cream

1	cup whipping cream
2	Tbsp. sugar
1	Tbsp. lemon zest
1	Tbsp. fresh lemon juice

So-Easy Chocolate Soufflés

Before cooking, run your thumb around the edges of the ramekins or measuring cups (see Step 3) to help the soufflés rise higher.

makes 2 servings
prep: 10 min. • **cook: 19 min.**

1   tsp. butter
1   Tbsp. granulated sugar
½   (4-oz.) semisweet chocolate
      baking bar
3   Tbsp. seedless strawberry jam
¾   tsp. vanilla extract
2   egg whites
Garnishes: powdered sugar,
      strawberries

1. Preheat oven to 350°. Grease bottom and sides of 2 (6-oz.) ramekins with butter. Lightly coat bottom and sides with granulated sugar, shaking out excess. Place ramekins on a baking sheet.

2. Microwave chocolate and jam in a small microwave-safe bowl at MEDIUM (50% power) 1 minute or until melted, stirring after 30 seconds. Stir in vanilla.

3. Beat egg whites at high speed with an electric mixer until soft peaks form. Stir about one-third of egg whites into chocolate mixture. Fold chocolate mixture into remaining egg whites. Spoon into ramekins. Run tip of thumb around edges of ramekins, wiping clean and creating a shallow indentation around outside edge of egg mixture.

4. Bake at 350° for 18 to 20 minutes or until soufflés rise and begin to brown on top. Garnish, if desired.

Note: We tested with Ghirardelli Semi-Sweet Chocolate Baking Bar.

Ice Cream & Frozen Desserts

Enjoy the lazy days of summer or any other season with one of these delicious frozen treats. Classics like Old-Fashioned Vanilla Ice Cream and Unbelievable Chocolate Ice Cream go hand-in-hand for the ultimate flavor combination. Top a few scoops with some banana slices, rainbow-colored sprinkles, and chocolate sauce for a delicious home-made sundae!

The Declaration of Independence was signed in 1776, but something else just as sweet happened in America that year—the first ice-cream parlor opened.

The history of ice cream is as scattered as sprinkles atop a sundae. From King Tang of Shang, China, who had a method of creating ice and milk concoctions, to the Roman emperor Nero demanding snow from nearby mountains to mix with his fruit drinks, ice cream's origin is international and diverse. In America, it is said that George Washington served the delectable dish to guests, as did Thomas Jefferson. In 1843, a housewife named Nancy Johnson invented the first ice-cream maker. Though she sold her creation to a local businessman, the new owner honored Nancy by calling the maker "Johnson Patent Ice-Cream Freezer." While there is some discrepancy as to which tale rings true as the origin of the ice-cream sundae, Two Rivers, Wisconsin is recognized by the Wisconsin State Historical Society as the true birthplace of the treat. Originally sold for a nickel, the chocolate-coated sundae created at Ed Berner's soda fountain became an instant hit. Although a nearby soda shop sold sundaes only on Sundays, when a little girl came and demanded a sundae on another day of the week, the proprietor couldn't help but consent. Thus, the sundae came into everyday existence.

Confections such as Old-Fashioned Vanilla Ice Cream, Simple Peach Sorbet, and Blueberry Sherbet bring sweet relief to sweltering Southern summers.

Old-Fashioned Vanilla Ice Cream

kids love it

Whether you use an old-fashioned hand-cranked ice-cream maker using ice and rock salt, or one of the new iceless, saltless, electric versions, let everyone have a hand in making the ice cream. Assign jobs to mix the ingredients, add salt or ice to the churn, or scoop the ice cream into serving bowls.

makes 3½ qt.
prep: 10 min. • **cook: 25 min.** • **other: 30 min.**

1. Combine first 3 ingredients in a large saucepan. Cook over low heat, stirring constantly, 25 to 30 minutes or until mixture thickens and coats a spoon; chill.

2. Stir in half-and-half and remaining ingredients; pour into freezer container of a 5- or 6-qt. hand-turned or electric freezer. Freeze according to manufacturer's instructions. (Instructions and freezing times may vary.)

3. Serve immediately, or spoon into an airtight container; freeze until firm.

6	large eggs, lightly beaten
2 ⅓	cups sugar
4	cups milk
2	cups half-and-half
¼	tsp. salt
2 ½	Tbsp. vanilla extract
3	cups whipping cream

Unbelievable Chocolate Ice Cream

kids love it

makes 1 gal.
prep: 15 min. • **other: 1 hr.**

1. Pour first 4 ingredients, and, if desired, cinnamon, into freezer container of a 5-qt. hand-turned or electric freezer. Freeze according to manufacturer's instructions. (Instructions and freezing times may vary.)

tip:
Freeze any leftover ice cream in an airtight container up to 2 months. Before sealing, place a sheet of plastic wrap directly on the ice cream's surface to prevent freezer burn.

½	gal. chocolate milk
1	(14-oz.) can sweetened condensed milk
1	(12-oz.) container frozen whipped topping, thawed
2	Tbsp. unsweetened cocoa
¼	tsp. ground cinnamon (optional)

Summertime Peach Ice Cream

Soft, ripe fruit lends the smoothest texture and most pronounced flavor to this warm-weather favorite.

makes 2 qt.
prep: 30 min. · **other: 1 hr., 30 min.**

4   cups peeled, diced fresh peaches (about 8 small ripe peaches)
1   cup sugar
1   (12-oz.) can evaporated milk
1   (3.4-oz.) package vanilla instant pudding mix
1   (14-oz.) can sweetened condensed milk
4   cups half-and-half
Garnish: mint sprigs

1. Combine peaches and sugar, and let stand 1 hour.

2. Process peach mixture in a food processor until smooth, stopping to scrape down sides.

3. Stir together evaporated milk and pudding mix in a large bowl; stir in peach purée, condensed milk, and half-and-half.

4. Pour mixture into freezer container of a 4-qt. hand-turned or electric freezer; freeze according to manufacturer's instructions. (Instructions and times may vary.) Spoon into an airtight container, and freeze until firm. Garnish, if desired.

Toffee-Coffee Ice-Cream Torte

makes 12 servings
prep: 30 min. • **cook: 4 min.** • **other: 8 hr.**

1. Line 2 (9- x 5-inch) loaf pans with plastic wrap, allowing excess to hang over sides.

2. Stir together 1 Tbsp. coffee liqueur and instant coffee granules until granules are dissolved. Combine coffee mixture, chocolate ice cream, and half of the chopped toffee in a large bowl. In a separate bowl, combine ½ gal. coffee ice cream and remaining chopped toffee. Spread half of chocolate ice-cream mixture evenly into 1 prepared loaf pan; top with half of coffee ice-cream mixture. Repeat layers in remaining loaf pan.

3. Brush ladyfingers with 3 Tbsp. coffee liqueur; place ladyfingers, brushed sides down, evenly over ice cream in loaf pans. Fold plastic wrap over to seal; freeze at least 8 hours.

4. Stir together brewed coffee, sugar, and cornstarch in a heavy saucepan over medium-high heat; cook, stirring constantly, until mixture starts to boil. Reduce heat to low, and cook 2 to 3 minutes or until thickened and clear. Remove from heat; cool. Stir in remaining 2 Tbsp. liqueur; cover and chill coffee sauce until ready to serve.

5. Invert tortes onto serving plates; remove and discard plastic wrap. Garnish, if desired. Serve with chilled coffee sauce.

Note: We tested with Hershey's Heath Toffee Bars.

6	Tbsp. coffee liqueur, divided
1	Tbsp. instant coffee granules
1	qt. chocolate ice cream, softened
1	(12-oz.) bag chocolate-covered toffee candy bars, finely chopped, divided
½	gal. coffee ice cream, softened
1	(3-oz.) package ladyfingers
1	cup strong-brewed coffee or espresso
½	cup sugar
1½	Tbsp. cornstarch

Garnishes: whipped topping, chopped toffee

kids love it

2   pt. vanilla ice cream, softened

15 mint-and-cream-filled chocolate
    sandwich cookies, chopped

1   (8.75-oz.) package large chewy
    chocolate cookies

Easy Chocolate-Mint Ice-Cream Sandwiches

This recipe uses packaged chewy cookies, but check your local bakery for freshly baked ones if you prefer.

makes 5 servings
prep: 15 min. • **other: 1 hr., 30 min.**

1. Stir together softened ice cream and sandwich cookie pieces. Freeze 30 minutes. Spread ice cream evenly on 1 side of 5 large chewy cookies; top with remaining large chewy cookies. Place in plastic or wax paper sandwich bags, and freeze at least 1 hour.

Note: We tested with Oreo Double Delight Mint'n Creme chocolate sandwich cookies and Archway Original Dutch Cocoa chocolate cookies.

Butter Pecan Ice-Cream Sandwiches: Omit mint-and-cream-filled sandwich cookies. Substitute 2 pt. butter pecan ice cream for vanilla ice cream and 1 (8.75-oz.) package large chewy sugar cookies for chewy chocolate cookies. Proceed as directed.

Mocha-Almond-Fudge Ice-Cream Sandwiches: Omit mint-and-cream-filled chocolate sandwich cookies. Substitute 2 pt. mocha-flavored ice cream with chocolate-covered almonds for vanilla ice cream. Proceed as directed. Note: We tested with Starbucks Coffee Almond Fudge Ice Cream.

Oatmeal-Rum-Raisin Ice-Cream Sandwiches: Omit mint-and-cream-filled sandwich cookies. Substitute 1 (8.75-oz.) package large chewy oatmeal cookies for chewy chocolate cookies. Pour ¼ cup dark rum over ½ cup golden raisins; let stand 2 hours. Drain and discard rum. Stir rum-soaked raisins into softened ice cream, and proceed as directed.

Strawberry-Buttermilk Sherbet

The tang of buttermilk balances the sweetness of the berries in this top-rated sherbet.

kids love it

makes about 8 servings
prep: 15 min. • **other: 3 hr.**

2   cups fresh strawberries
2   cups buttermilk
1   cup sugar
1   tsp. vanilla extract
Garnish: fresh mint sprigs

1. Process strawberries in a food processor or blender 30 seconds or until smooth, stopping to scrape down sides. Pour strawberry puree through a fine wire-mesh strainer into a large bowl, pressing with back of a spoon. Discard solids. Add buttermilk, sugar, and vanilla to puree; stir until well blended. Cover and chill 1 hour.

2. Pour strawberry mixture into freezer container of a 1½-qt. electric ice-cream maker, and freeze according to manufacturer's instructions. (Instructions and freezing times may vary.) Garnish, if desired.

Note: 1 (16-oz.) package frozen strawberries, thawed, may be substituted for fresh strawberries.

If it's summer in the South, then there is a blueberry festival nearby. Check for festivals in June in Alabama, Georgia, Mississippi, North Carolina, Florida, and Texas. Virginia and Maryland host their festivals in July.

Blueberry Sherbet

This easy and flavorful dessert calls for just 5 ingredients, a pan, your freezer, and a blender.

makes 6 servings
prep: 15 min. • **other: 8 hr.**

2   cups fresh or frozen blueberries, thawed
1   cup nonfat buttermilk
½   cup sugar
1   Tbsp. fresh lemon juice
½   tsp. vanilla extract
Garnish: fresh mint sprig

1. Process first 5 ingredients in a blender until smooth. Pour mixture into a 9-inch square pan; cover and freeze 4 hours or until firm.

2. Break frozen blueberry mixture into chunks using a fork. Process frozen mixture, in batches, in a blender until smooth. Cover and freeze 4 hours or until frozen. Garnish, if desired.

tip:
A food processor fitted with the knife blade works just as well as a blender to blend this icy concoction. With either appliance, stop and scrape down the sides as needed.

Simple Peach Sorbet

It has just 3 ingredients, yet this satiny sorbet has an intense ripe peach flavor that belies its simplicity. This sorbet is as creamy as ice cream, but without the milk. In fact, sorbet was made from snow 1,000 years before the first ice cream was created.

makes 4 cups
prep: 5 min. • **other: 3 hr., 10 min.**

1. Process all ingredients in a blender until smooth, stopping to scrape down sides. Pour mixture into a 9-inch square pan. Cover and freeze 3 hours or until firm.

2. Remove pan from freezer; let stand 10 minutes. Break frozen mixture into chunks; process in a food processor until smooth.

4	or 5 fresh ripe peaches, peeled and chopped
¾	cup sugar
1	tsp. fresh lemon juice

tip:

If fresh peaches are out of season, substitute a 16-oz. bag of frozen sliced peaches.

Blueberry-Lime Granita

makes 7 servings
prep: 15 min. • **other: 8 hr., 5 min.**

2 cups blueberries
½ cup sugar
½ tsp. lime zest
2 tsp. fresh lime juice
3 cups diet lemon-lime soft drink, chilled
Garnish: lime rind twists

1. Process blueberries in a food processor or blender until smooth, stopping to scrape down sides. Add sugar, lime zest, and lime juice; process until well blended. Pour into an 11- x 7-inch baking dish. Stir in soft drink. Cover and freeze 8 hours. Remove from freezer; let stand 5 minutes.

2. Chop mixture into large chunks, and place in food processor in batches; pulse 5 to 6 times or until mixture is smooth. Serve immediately, or freeze until ready to serve. Garnish, if desired.

Key Lime Frozen Yogurt

Serve this refreshing dessert with fresh raspberries or blackberries, pressed between graham crackers or gingersnaps, or on its own for a tangy treat.

makes 12 servings
prep: 5 min. • **other: 30 min.**

1 (32-oz.) container whole milk French vanilla yogurt
1 (14-oz.) can fat-free sweetened condensed milk
½ cup Key lime juice

1. Whisk together all ingredients in a large mixing bowl until well blended. Pour mixture into freezer container of a 1½-qt. electric ice-cream maker, and freeze according to manufacturer's instructions. (Instructions and freezing times may vary.) Cover and freeze until desired firmness.

Note: We tested with Stonyfield Farm Organic Whole Milk French Vanilla Yogurt and Nellie & Joe's Famous Key West Lime Juice.

Test Kitchens' Guide to Successful Baking

The Food staff spends a lot of time in the kitchen, personally and professionally, so good tools are high on our must-have lists. Whether you're a beginner or a seasoned pro, the equipment guide and tips for baking on the following pages will help you achieve baking perfection.

Essential Baking Equipment

Heavy-duty electric stand mixer. It comes with attachments: a paddle, a dough hook, and a whisk-like wire beater. We test with KitchenAid mixers.

Liquid measuring cups. Glass measuring cups with a pouring spout are best for liquids. Do not use to measure dry ingredients such as flour; you'll end up with at least an extra Tbsp. per cup. This can negatively affect the moistness of your baked goods.

Nested measuring cups. Dry ingredients are measured using a set of graduated cups ranging from ⅛ or ¼ cup to 1 cup; they're usually made from plastic or metal.

Tart pans. These are shallow and usually have fluted sides and can be round, square, or rectangular; they are made of dark metal or tinned steel. Common sizes are 10 inches and 11 inches.

Food processor. A handy substitute for a blender, it makes easy work of chopping nuts and chocolate, as well as mixing up homemade piecrusts. The larger ones (11- to 14-cup) are the most versatile.

Rolling pin. It's used for rolling pie, tart, biscuit, or cinnamon roll dough. Most home bakers prefer ones with handles on both ends.

Ceramic pie weights. These prevent a prebaked pie crust from forming large air bubbles.

Pie crust shield. It's placed over the pie while baking to prevent over-browning.

Pie plates. Made from glass, ceramic, or metal, these are commonly available in 9-inch and 10-inch sizes. (It's best to also purchase a deep-dish size as an option.) Glass is generally preferred for even browning, plus it allows you to see how the bottom of the crust is baking.

Cooling rack. A wire rack allows air to circulate evenly on all sides of freshly baked cakes, pies, or cookies. It's handy to have two or three cooling racks, especially when baking multiple cake layers or large batches of cookies.

Muffin pan. Sizes come in 6 or 12 cups and vary from miniature to jumbo. You can purchase nonstick, steel, or aluminum.

Bundt pan. It has a central tube and fluted sides with a fixed bottom. Make sure you grease and flour Bundt pans well to ensure proper release. Double-check the size by filling it to the rim with cups of water. Depending on the brand, a 10-inch pan may hold 10, 12, or 14 cups.

Tube pan. It has a central tube with straight sides. It is best to choose light rather than dark metal for better browning results. Refer to Bundt pan (above) on how to measure the pan.

Rubber spatula. Use it to scrape batters from bowls into baking pans or to spread fillings.

Baking cups. These line cups in a muffin pan to prevent sticking and offer an attractive appearance. Most are made of paper or aluminum foil.

Candy thermometer. It allows you to cook mixtures to precise temperatures. Purchase one that has an adjustable clip so it can be attached to the side of a saucepan.

Pastry brush. It's great for brushing crumbs from a cake or cake stand. Invest in a high-quality natural bristle brush to keep stray bristles from shedding into food.

Nested measuring spoons. A set of graduated sizes ranges from 1/8 tsp. to 1 Tbsp. and is usually made of plastic or metal.

Wire whisk. Keep varying sizes and shapes of this tool on hand. Balloon whisks are useful in baking because they incorporate more air into egg whites and cream.

Wire-mesh strainer. Use this to sift dry ingredients, such as powdered sugar, over a dessert or to strain solids from a sauce.

Cookie scoop. Found in assorted sizes, it's perfect for scooping muffin batter into pans.

Assorted silicone spatulas. Be sure to have different sizes and shapes on hand. They are extremely flexible, and many are heat-resistant.

Sifter. Usually made of metal, it removes lumps from flour or powdered sugar.

Microplane grater. Modeled after a woodworker's plane, this handy utensil is used to grate chocolate and citrus zest with ease.

Off-set spatula. This slightly flexible baking utensil is designed to keep hands away from food when spreading frosting or filling on baked goods. Select one with a blade that is made of stainless steel.

Silicone basting and pastry brush. It's a newer product that cleans up beautifully in the dishwasher and won't hold onto food odors or shed bristles into food.

Cake pans. You should have sets of three in at least two sizes, 8 inches and 9 inches.

Jelly-roll pan. It has shallow sides and is used to make sponge-type cakes that are filled or rolled. The most common size is 15 x 10 inches.

Loaf pans. Purchase these in a variety of sizes—from 5 x 3 inches to 8 x 4 inches. The standard size is usually 9 x 5 inches. Smaller sizes are great for baking gift-size loaves for sharing.

13- x 9-inch pan. This is the most versatile pan in a cook's collection. It's just right for sheet cakes, brownies, and casseroles.

Springform pans. These are deep, round metal pans with sides that clamp shut for baking and expand when clamp is released after baking. The most common sizes are 9 inches and 10 inches.

Wooden spoon. Use it to stir heavy or dense mixtures. Choose one that is strong enough not to split or crack.

Mixing bowls. Having several bowls in a range of sizes and materials is helpful.

Handheld electric mixer. It's perfect for mixing lighter batters or using with a double boiler or saucepan on the cooktop.

Tips for Perfect Pies & Cakes

Pointers for Better Pies

• **Use refrigerated and frozen piecrusts** before the expiration date printed on the package. Choose the freshest package available at the supermarket.

• **If your piecrust tears,** dampen the torn edges, and gently press them back together. Problem solved.

• **When preparing a single-crust pie,** fold excess dough underneath itself, even level with the pie plate's rim, and crimp.

Pie Troubleshooting

You may experience these common problems while baking pies. Don't despair; we've included some fixes and information about how to avoid additional mistakes. Always remember, a dollop of fresh whipped cream or a scoop of ice cream can cover up most visible flaws.

• **If the piecrust shrinks,** the pastry was stretched too tightly. To avoid shrinkage, chill briefly before baking, and add pie weights when prebaking.

• **If the filling bubbles over,** the pie may be too full, the pie plate may not be deep enough, or the filling could contain too much liquid and needs to be thickened with additional starch. Place an aluminum foil-lined baking sheet beneath the pie to catch messy drips.

• **If the top crust of double-crust pie sags,** the pie may not have enough filling or the dish could be too deep. Top slices with ice cream before serving.

Cake Freezing Guide

• **For the freshest taste,** it's best to bake and freeze unfrosted cake layers and pound cakes. Cakes shrink when frozen and expand when thawed, which can cause the frosting to crack.

• **Place baked, completely cooled,** unfrosted cake layers on baking sheets, and freeze until firm. Wrap each frozen layer in plastic wrap and aluminum foil, and place in large zip-top plastic freezer bags; freeze up to one month. Thaw at room temperature. (Try filling and frosting the cake layers while they're still partially frozen—this makes for super-easy spreading with no crumbs.)

Cake Troubleshooting

Baking cakes can be tricky, so we've put together a list of routine things that can go wrong, along with possible reasons, and how to prevent them from happening again. These simple steps will guarantee baking success.

Top of cake is domed or cracked:	Cake is dense; texture is heavy:	Cake collapses or sinks in the middle:	Crust is sticky:	Batter overflowed:
• Removed from pan too soon. • Too much baking soda or baking powder was added. • Not enough sugar was incorporated. • Too many eggs or too much liquid was added to batter. • Pan placed too close to top heating element in oven.	• Too much flour was incorporated. • Pan may have been too small. • Oven temperature too low. • Egg whites were overbeaten.	• Removed from oven too soon, not completely baked. • Oven temperature too high. • Opened oven door before cake structure was set. • Added too much baking soda, baking powder, liquid, or sugar.	• Added too much sugar. • Under-baked. • Oven temperature too low.	• Added too much baking soda, baking powder, or beaten egg whites. • Overmixed batter. • Pan used was too small for amount of batter.

Pound Cake Perfection

Here are some of our insider tips for turning out a perfect pound cake.

1 **Carefully read through the entire recipe,** and prepare any special ingredients, such as chopped fruits or toasted nuts, before mixing the batter.

2 **Prepare the recipe as directed,** and use name-brand ingredients. Store brands of sugar are often more finely ground than name brands, yielding more sugar per cup, which can cause the cake to fall. Store brands of butter may contain more liquid fat, and flours more hard wheat, making the cake heavy.

3 **Measure accurately.** Be sure to use dry measuring cups for flour and sugar. Spoon flour into the cups and lightly level with the straight edge of a small offset spatula or knife. Extra sugar or leavening causes a cake to fall; extra flour makes it dry.

4 **For maximum volume,** have ingredients at room temperature. We like to premeasure our ingredients and assemble them in the order listed. That way, if interrupted, we're less likely to make a mistake.

5 **Beat softened butter** (and cream cheese or vegetable shortening) at medium speed with an electric mixer until creamy. This can take from 1 to 7 minutes, depending on the power of your mixer. Gradually add sugar, continuing to beat until light and fluffy. These steps are important because they whip air into the cake batter so it will rise during baking.

6 **Add eggs, one at a time,** beating just until the yolk disappears. Overbeating the eggs may cause the batter to overflow the sides of the pan during baking or create a fragile crust that crumbles and separates from the cake as it cools.

7 **To prevent the batter from curdling,** always add the dry ingredients alternately with the liquid, beginning and ending with the dry ingredients. Mix just until blended after each addition. Overmixing the batter once the flour has been added creates a tough, rubbery cake.

8 **Be sure to use the correct type of cake pan.** Pound cake recipes calling for a tube pan won't always fit in a Bundt pan. (Tube pans have straight, high sides, while Bundt pans are more shallow and fluted.) Although both may measure 10 inches in diameter, each holds a different amount of batter. We also found that some 10-inch tube pans hold 12 cups of batter while others hold 14 or 16 cups. The same pound cake recipe rises and bakes differently in each pan. When unsure of size, use a cup measure to fill the cake pan with water to determine the pan's capacity.

9 **Grease cake pans** with solid vegetable shortening, such as Crisco, and always dust with flour—a slippery surface keeps the batter from rising to its full volume.

10 **Use an oven thermometer** to check your oven's temperature for accuracy. Many home ovens bake hotter or cooler than the temperatures to which they're set.

11 **Place the cake pan** in the center of the oven, and keep the door closed until the minimum baking time has elapsed. If the cake requires more baking, gently close the oven door as soon as possible after testing to prevent jarring and loss of heat—both can cause a cake to fall if it's not done.

12 **Test for doneness** by inserting a long wooden pick into the center of the cake. It should come out clean, with no batter or wet crumbs clinging to it. (Some cakes will have a crack in the center that appears wet even when fully cooked, so avoid this area when testing.)

13 **After removing from the oven,** place the pound cake, right side up, in the pan on a wire rack, and let cool for 10 minutes away from drafts. This allows the cake to become firm enough to remove from the pan without breaking apart. Cooling too long in the pan will cause the cake to be damp and stick to the pan. Remove pound cake from pan to wire rack, and let cool completely.

metric equivalents

The recipes that appear in this cookbook use the standard U.S. method for measuring liquid and dry or solid ingredients (teaspoons, tablespoons, and cups). The information in the following charts is provided to help cooks outside the United States successfully use these recipes. All equivalents are approximate.

Metric Equivalents for Different Types of Ingredients

A standard cup measure of a dry or solid ingredient will vary in weight depending on the type of ingredient. A standard cup of liquid is the same volume for any type of liquid. Use the following chart when converting standard cup measures to grams (weight) or milliliters (volume).

Standard Cup	Fine Powder (ex. flour)	Grain (ex. rice)	Granular (ex. sugar)	Liquid Solids (ex. butter)	Liquid (ex. milk)
1	140 g	150 g	190 g	200 g	240 ml
¾	105 g	113 g	143 g	150 g	180 ml
⅔	93 g	100 g	125 g	133 g	160 ml
½	70 g	75 g	95 g	100 g	120 ml
⅓	47 g	50 g	63 g	67 g	80 ml
¼	35 g	38 g	48 g	50 g	60 ml
⅛	18 g	19 g	24 g	25 g	30 ml

Useful Equivalents for Dry Ingredients by Weight

(To convert ounces to grams, multiply the number of ounces by 30.)

1 oz	=	¹⁄₁₆ lb	=	30 g
4 oz	=	¼ lb	=	120 g
8 oz	=	½ lb	=	240 g
12 oz	=	¾ lb	=	360 g
16 oz	=	1 lb	=	480 g

Useful Equivalents for Length

(To convert inches to centimeters, multiply the number of inches by 2.5.)

1 in					=	2.5 cm		
6 in	=	½ ft			=	15 cm		
12 in	=	1 ft			=	30 cm		
36 in	=	3 ft	=	1 yd	=	90 cm		
40 in					=	100 cm	=	1 m

Useful Equivalents for Liquid Ingredients by Volume

¼ tsp					=	1 ml	
½ tsp					=	2 ml	
1 tsp					=	5 ml	
3 tsp	=	1 Tbsp			=	½ fl oz	= 15 ml
		2 Tbsp	=	⅛ cup	=	1 fl oz	= 30 ml
		4 Tbsp	=	¼ cup	=	2 fl oz	= 60 ml
		5⅓ Tbsp	=	⅓ cup	=	3 fl oz	= 80 ml
		8 Tbsp	=	½ cup	=	4 fl oz	= 120 ml
		10⅔ Tbsp	=	⅔ cup	=	5 fl oz	= 160 ml
		12 Tbsp	=	¾ cup	=	6 fl oz	= 180 ml
		16 Tbsp	=	1 cup	=	8 fl oz	= 240 ml
		1 pt	=	2 cups	=	16 fl oz	= 480 ml
		1 qt	=	4 cups	=	32 fl oz	= 960 ml
						33 fl oz	= 1000 ml = 1 l

Useful Equivalents for Cooking/Oven Temperatures

	Fahrenheit	Celsius	Gas Mark
Freeze water	32° F	0° C	
Room temperature	68° F	20° C	
Boil water	212° F	100° C	
Bake	325° F	160° C	3
	350° F	180° C	4
	375° F	190° C	5
	400° F	200° C	6
	425° F	220° C	7
	450° F	230° C	8
Broil			Grill

index

Sauces & Glazes

Sheet Cakes

Sweet Breads & Coffee Cakes

Tarts